Alcohol and Drug Counselor Exam Practice Problems:

450 Practice Questions for the IC&RC ADC Exam

Bova Books LLC
Study More Efficiently

BovaBooks@gmail.com

The contents of this book are for educational purposes only and in no way shall be used as reference for professional opinion. No liability will be assumed by the author and the information in this book shall not be used in a court of law.

Contents

Exam Format and Expectations

Hello and thank you for your purchase. We are here for all of your studying needs on your way to certification. Please be sure to email us at BovaBooks@gmail.com for any questions you may have.

Our main goal when developing our study material is to focus your studying on the core concepts you need to know on test day. We develop our material based closely on the syllabus provided by IC&RC so you no longer have to waste time sieving through unnecessary material. Here is a breakdown of what to expect from the exam:

- The examination is multiple-choice with three or four options.

- You are often asked for the "best" or "most likely" answer for each question. Be sure to keep this in mind as you eliminate possible answers.

- Be sure to answer every question since there is no penalty for guessing.

- There are 150 questions on the exam

- 25 of the questions are not scored, however you will not know which these are so treat all of them as if they are real

The exam is divided into four separate domains to determine which topics are necessary. We suggest reviewing the syllabus thoroughly and identifying any areas where you may need additional studying. The breakdown of the questions is as follows:

Domains Weight on Exam

Domain I: Screening, Assessment, and Engagement 23%

Domain II: Treatment Planning, Collaboration, and Referral 27%

Domain III: Counseling 28%

Domain IV: Professional and Ethical Responsibilities 22%

Domain I: Screening, Assessment, and Engagement

- **Task 1: Demonstrate verbal and non-verbal communication to establish rapport and promote engagement.**

- **Task 2: Discuss with the client the rationale, purpose, and procedures associated with the screening and assessment process to facilitate client understanding and cooperation.**

- **Task 3: Assess client's immediate needs by evaluating observed behavior and other relevant information including signs and symptoms of intoxication and withdrawal.**

- **Task 4: Administer appropriate evidence-based screening and assessment instruments specific to clients to determine their strengths and needs.**

- **Task 5: Obtain relevant history and related information from the client and other pertinent sources to establish eligibility and appropriateness of services.**

- **Task 6: Screen for physical needs, medical conditions, and co-occurring mental health disorders that might require additional assessment and referral.**

- **Task 7: Interpret results of screening and assessment and integrate all available information to formulate diagnostic impression and determine an appropriate course of action.**

- **Task 8: Develop a written summary of the results of the screening and assessment to document and support the diagnostic impressions and treatment recommendations.**

Domain II: Treatment Planning, Collaboration, and Referral

- **Task 1: Formulate and discuss diagnostic assessment and recommendations with the client**

- **Task 2: Use ongoing assessment and collaboration with the client and concerned others to review and modify the treatment plan to address treatment needs.**

- **Task 3: Match client needs with community resources to facilitate positive client outcomes.**

- **Task 4: Discuss rationale for a referral with the client.**

- **Task 5: Communicate with community resources regarding needs of the client.**

- **Task 6: Advocate for the client in areas of identified needs to facilitate continuity of care.**

- **Task 7: Evaluate the effectiveness of case management activities to ensure quality service coordination.**

- **Task 8: Develop a plan with the client to strengthen ongoing recovery outside of primary treatment.**

- **Task 9: Document treatment progress, outcomes, and continuing care plans.**

- **Task 10: Utilize multiple pathways of recovery in treatment planning and referral.**

Domain III: Counseling

- **Task 1: Develop a therapeutic relationship with clients, families, and concerned others to facilitate transition into the recovery process.**

- **Task 2: Provide information to the client regarding the structure, expectations, and purpose of the counseling process.**

- **Task 3: Continually evaluate the client's safety, relapse potential, and the need for crisis intervention.**

- **Task 4: Apply evidence-based, culturally competent counseling strategies and modalities to facilitate progress towards completion of treatment objectives.**

- **Task 5: Assist families and concerned others in understanding substance use disorders and engage them in the recovery process.**

- **Task 6: Document counseling activity and progress towards treatment goals and objectives.**

- **Task 7: Provide information on issues of identity, ethnic background, age, sexual orientation, and gender as it relates to substance use, prevention and recovery.**

- **Task 8: Provide information about the disease of addiction and the related health and psychosocial consequences.**

Domain IV: Professional and Ethical Responsibilities

- Task 1: Adhere to established professional codes of ethics and standards of practice to uphold client rights while promoting best interests of the client and profession.

- Task 2: Recognize diversity and client demographics, culture and other factors influencing behavior to provide services that are sensitive to the uniqueness of the individual.

- Task 3: Continue professional development through education, self-evaluation, clinical supervision, and consultation to maintain competence and enhance professional effectiveness.

- Task 4: Identify and evaluate client needs that are outside of the counselor's ethical scope of practice and refer to other professionals as appropriate.

- Task 5: Uphold client's rights to privacy and confidentiality according to best practices in preparation and handling of records.

- Task 6: Obtain written consent to release information from the client and/or legal guardian, according to best practices.

Practice Problems

Question 1

A fourteen-year-old male is being evaluated for cocaine abuse. He has no knowledge of any family history of abuse and has indicated that he began only in the past 6 months. Which of the following addiction factors is most likely the most influential on his drug use?

(A) Family influence
(B) Genetics
(C) Peer influence
(D) Television and media

b/c he is adolecent

Question 2

Which of the following is not a model for the causation of addiction?

(A) Moral model
(B) Blended model
(C) Genetic model
(D) Familial model

Question 3

As an individual continues to use an addictive forming drug over a period of time, which of the following is a correct statement regarding the influence of outside factors (peers, family, stress) contributing the habit of addiction?

(A) As drug use continues the influence of outside factors remains about the same
(B) As drug use continues the influence of outside factors increases
(C) As drug use continues the influence of outside factors decreases
(D) None of the above

Question 4

Which of the following is the most commonly abused substance in America?

(A) Marijuana
(B) Alcohol
(C) Cocaine
(D) Prescription Drugs

Question 5

Which of the following is a true statement regarding the abuse of alcohol?

(A) Women have a higher risk of developing problems from alcohol abuse than men
(B) Men are more likely to drink higher volumes of alcohol than women
(C) Organ damage due to alcohol abuse is more likely in women than men
(D) All of the above

Question 6

Which of the following a false statement about marijuana use?

(A) Marijuana is not an addictive substance
(B) Marijuana can contribute to depression and suicide
(C) Research shows Marijuana users generally have a lower level of fulfillment in life
(D) Marijuana increases the risk of heart disease

Question 7

Which of the following is not an example of prescription drug abuse?

(A) A friend providing OxyContin for a stiff neck
(B) Taking an additional Valium beyond the amount prescribed to ease tension before public speaking
(C) Using leftover Vicodin from a car accident that occurred a year prior to treat a new injury
(D) None of the above

Question 8

Which of the following is most commonly the main reason for a client deciding to begin the process of treatment?

(A) Internal motivation
(B) Family or Peer encouragement
(C) Diagnosed medical issues
(D) Financial issues

Question 9

Which of the following is not an effective technique for establishing rapport with a client during the initial interview?

(A) Observing and noting the dress and appearance of the client
(B) Providing reassurance that things will be ok no matter how dire the individual's situation
(C) Exhibit acceptance regardless of the client's prior actions
(D) Use of open-ended questions

Question 10

Which of the following is not an example of proper active listening?

(A) Restating specific words the client has used
(B) Refocusing the client's attention on a specific topic of interest
(C) Providing stories from your own experience that relate to the client's struggle
(D) Summarizing key feelings that the client has shared

Question 11

Which of the following is not a part of the screening process?

(A) Identify the presence of a problem
(B) Identify the likely solution to problem
(C) Measuring the severity of an identified problem
(D) Identify the need for further evaluation

Question 12

Which of the following is not an example of an effective screening processes?

(A) Evaluating the subject in multiple locations
(B) Evaluating the subject by gathering information from multiple people
(C) In-depth initial screening questions to provide a thorough process
(D) Obtaining information from multiple sources

Question 13

Which of the following is a screening instrument for co-occurring disorders?

(A) Modified Mini-Screen (MMS)
(B) Michigan Alcohol Screening Test (MAST)
(C) CAGE Questionnaire
(D) Global Appraisal of Individual Needs (GAIN)

Question 14

Which of the following withdrawal symptoms is common in nearly all types of drugs when use is stopped?

(A) Seizures
(B) Itchy feeling all over skin
(C) Dysphoria
(D) Delirium Tremens

Question 15

Which of the following is not one of the eight stages of effect for alcohol?

(A) Euphoria
(B) Confusion
(C) Depression
(D) Coma

Question 16

A client in an initial screening indicates that she has not slept very well at all in weeks and seems to be suffering from a reduced appetite. You notice she has a noticeable bruise on her leg and when asked about it she recalls a physical altercation she had recently at a party. When consulting her mother, she mentions that her mood has been very unpredictable and that she would often storm out unexpectedly. Which of the following drugs is the subject most likely suffering withdrawal symptoms from?

(A) Methamphetamine
(B) MDMA
(C) Cocaine
(D) Steroids

Question 17

Which of the following assessment instrument format is the most appropriate for a 45-year old woman who has an addiction to alcohol and is recently divorced? The woman has a single child and will be entering into a custody battle with her previous husband.

(A) Standardized Interview
(B) Structured Interview
(C) Self-administered test
(D) None of the above

Question 18

Which of the following is not a characteristic of self-administered assessment tests?

(A) They most often are written at a 4th or 5th grade reading level
(B) They provide a quantifiable metric
(C) They prevent interviewer bias
(D) They must be administered by highly skilled staff

Question 19

Which of the following is an acceptable person for the use of a translator for an assessment involving a low English proficient client?

(A) Family member
(B) A community insider
(C) Independent translator
(D) All of the above

Question 20

A client enters and shows visual signs of withdrawal. They appear to have significant nausea, agitation, and are indicating the intention for self-inflicted harm. Which of the following is the most appropriate initial reaction?

(A) Attempt to calm the client and begin an initial assessment
(B) Alert the clients friends and family
(C) Seek medical attention for the client
(D) All of the above

Question 21

Which of the following is not a factor in the assessment for suicide risk?

(A) Abuse of alcohol
(B) Family history of suicide
(C) Evidence of aggression towards others
(D) None of the above

Question 22

Which of the following drug test types is not appropriate for the use of monitoring compliance on a regular basis?

(A) Hair
(B) Urine
(C) Saliva
(D) Sweat

Question 23

Which of the following ranges is the amount of time alcohol stays in the body after ingestion?

(A) A few hours
(B) 12 to 24 hrs.
(C) 1 to 3 days
(D) About a week

Question 24

Which of the following is not linked to causing false positives on drug tests?

(A) Doxylamine
(B) Poppy seeds
(C) Sesame seeds
(D) Sertraline

Question 25

Which of the following is most often not a step for counselors in the assessment of co-occurring disorders?

(A) Screening of co-occurring disorder
(B) Determine the severity of the potential disorder
(C) Diagnose the mental disorder
(D) Determine the effect the disability has on the client in relation to substance abuse

Question 26

Which of the following is not a true statement regarding the connection between mental health disorders and substance abuse?

(A) The effect of drug use is equal for those with or without mental health disorders despite the increased risk
(B) An undiagnosed mental health issue can lead to substance abuse
(C) Some drugs may cause diagnosable mental illness after extended use
(D) The risk of mental health disorders can be increased with drug abuse

Question 27

Which of the following is not consistent with the methodologies for the American Psychiatric Association DSM-5 criteria?

(A) All people are not automatically susceptible to developing substance abuse disorders
(B) The brain's reaction to drugs of creating a rewarding feeling is an essential part of the substance abuse process
(C) Substance induced disorders may be a result of a preexisting condition
(D) Not all people are equally susceptible to substance abuse

Question 28

Which of the following is not an example of a substance use disorder?

(A) A person leaving work early due to the need for drug use
(B) Constantly saying they need to cut down on use but never managing to do so
(C) Entering into knowingly dangerous situations to obtain the drugs
(D) Having feelings of severe depression

Question 29

In evaluating a client using the DSM-5 criteria, you note that they show symptoms of five of the eleven SUD criteria. Which of the following is the severity of the substance abuse disorder?

(A) No diagnostic of SUD
(B) Mild
(C) Moderate
(D) Severe

Question 30

Which of the following substances is most likely to be associated with withdrawal symptoms of increased physical activity such as elevated blood pressure, agitation and anxiety?

(A) Cocaine
(B) Alcohol
(C) Ecstasy
(D) Steroids

Question 31

After an assessment and medical examination, the client is diagnosed with having long-term damage to their ability to concentrate and memory. Which of the following is most likely the substance of abuse?

(A) Amphetamines
(B) Heroin
(C) Marijuana
(D) Steroids

Question 32

Which of the following is not a characteristic of the intake process?

(A) It is the first phase of the treatment process
(B) It may involve any significant others of the client
(C) It mostly serves a more administrative than clinical function
(D) The intake process is standardized according to the institution of use

Question 33

Which of the following is not a basic function of the intake process?

(A) Determine if the client in fact needs service
(B) Collection of data
(C) Determine a plan for treatment
(D) All of the above

Question 34

Which of the following is not a reason for confidential information to be released as per a client's right to confidentiality?

(A) By authorization of a significant other
(B) To report child abuse
(C) For a medical emergency
(D) If the court determines a "good cause"

Question 35

Which of the following is not a lawful right of the client?

(A) Right to Individual Dignity
(B) Right to Communication
(C) Right to Personal Effects
(D) Right to Minimum Level of Service

Question 36

Which of the following is not a proper characteristic of the development of a treatment plan?

(A) A treatment plan can be developed concurrently with the late stages of diagnosis
(B) The client's needs should be prioritized according to the urgency of the concern
(C) Treatment plans are individualized to the client's needs
(D) Treatment plans require regular review for adjustments

Question 37

Which of the following is not a typical phase of the treatment process?

(A) Engagement
(B) Detoxification
(C) Stabilization
(D) Primary Treatment

Question 38

Collaboration with the client is an important part of the treatment process. Which of the following is a not an appropriate way to engage the client?

(A) Have the client determine their appropriate treatment or diagnosis
(B) Review identified strengths and concerns with the client
(C) Review proposed goals of the treatment process
(D) Have the client sign off on the treatment plan

Question 39

Which of the following occurrences typically warrants the development of a new treatment plan?

(A) Any time there is change in service
(B) When the client achieves a specified goal
(C) A client who is readmitted to treatment
(D) Any time the client has had a setback

Question 40

Which of the following is not a stage of change as recognized in the DiClemente and Prochaska Model of Change?

(A) Contemplation
(B) Acceptance
(C) Action
(D) Termination

Question 41

If a client fails to improve or if the situation continues to deteriorate, which of the following is the most appropriate course of action?

(A) Re-evaluate the treatment plan and make adjustments based on the individual
(B) Re-conduct the screening process
(C) Interview the client to determine what is not working
(D) None of the above

Question 42

Which of the following is not an ASAM criteria for the documentation of a treatment plan?

(A) Problems or priorities must be identified
(B) Specified time intervals for assessment of the treatment process
(C) Realistic goals identified
(D) The progress made must be measured

Question 43

Which of the following is most often included in the individualized treatment plan but not the initial treatment plan?

(A) Problem identified
(B) Goals
(C) Objectives
(D) Diagnosis

Question 44

Which of the following is not a true statement regarding goals and objectives as defined in an individual treatment plan?

(A) Goals should be broad
(B) Objectives should be broad
(C) Goals should be measurable
(D) Objectives should be measurable

Question 45

After a relapse, what stage of change is the client most likely to return to?

(A) Preparation
(B) Contemplation
(C) Action
(D) Maintenance

Question 46

What is not a true characteristic of the methodology behind the stages of change model?

(A) There are five distinct stages
(B) Clients may move back and forth between stages
(C) Clients move through the stages linearly
(D) Relapses are to be expected and are common

Question 47

Which of the following defines the mental state of a client who is ready to enter into the preparation stage of change?

(A) The person recognizes there is a problem with how substances have affected their life
(B) The person has had adverse experiences directly related to substance abuse
(C) The person can recognize that the disadvantages of continuing substance abuse outweigh any perceived advantages
(D) The person is prepared to decide on how to change

Question 48

During which stage of change do withdrawal symptoms most often occur?

(A) Contemplation
(B) Preparation
(C) Action
(D) Maintenance

Question 49

Which of the following is most often the biggest source of disagreement during collaboration efforts amongst agencies?

(A) Use of differing assessment tools
(B) Agreement of treatment plan
(C) Timeline of events
(D) Which agency is primary

Question 50

What is not a role of a primary agency during collaboration?

(A) Provide an all-inclusive assessment for use by all agencies
(B) Designate the primary contact
(C) Determine all final assessments
(D) None of the above

Question 51

Which of the following is not a main objective of case management systems?

(A) Accessibility
(B) Accountability
(C) Consistency of care
(D) None of the above

Question 52

What is not a main element of establishing a case management system?

(A) Primary Screener
(B) Case Manager
(C) Core Agency
(D) None of the above

Question 53

Which of the following is not an established approach to case management for any aspect of the process?

(A) Intensive
(B) High Intensity
(C) Brokerage
(D) Integrated

Question 54

What statement below would not be consistent with the established principles of case management?

(A) A client should lead in determining which resources presented are appropriate
(B) Case management should remain firm on prior established processes
(C) Case management will determine the appropriate action of intervening if problems arise
(D) Case management ensures that a client's individual strengths are emphasized as a part of the process

Question 55

Case management involves the advocacy of the client as needed. What situation below is not an example of this?

(A) Educating other agencies about substance abuse
(B) Lobby to adjust agency procedures for the individual if appropriate
(C) Lobby to law enforcement against any sanctions on the client
(D) Informing family members of the process

Question 56

Which of the following is not a key element in the development of cultural competency as per Cross et al., 1989?

(A) Valuing diversity
(B) Make a cultural self-assessment
(C) Understanding and awareness of cultural differences
(D) Incorporating cultural knowledge

Question 57

Case management should be pragmatic to ensure the client's needs are met so that there is a foundation of living for treatment. Which of the following is not consistent with the intention of this aspect of case management?

(A) Ensuring the client has suitable food and water
(B) Ensuring a stable living situation for an extended period of time before treatment
(C) Taking action for the health and safety of a client's child
(D) Teaching a client necessary daily skills

Question 58

A case manager should have all of the following essential characteristics to ensure an effective process except:

(A) Ability to recognize substance abuse
(B) Ability to establish rapport
(C) Awareness of appropriate boundaries
(D) A non-judgmental approach

Question 59

When referring a client, which of the following is not true about the process?

(A) The client should always initiate and follow up on the referral themselves
(B) Rationale for the referral should be thoroughly explained
(C) Continue to evaluate the referral as the client progress

Question 60

Referrals by substance abuse agencies are typically made to all the following except:

(A) Marriage counselors
(B) Physical therapy
(C) Religious support
(D) Financial counseling

Question 61

Which of the following is not an essential item in a comprehensive service plan?

(A) Long term goals
(B) Short term goals
(C) Writeup of the current status
(D) Required services for the client

Question 62

All of the following are common problems that may arise with referrals except:

(A) Client dropout
(B) Eligibility requirements
(C) Incomplete client information
(D) All of the above

Question 63

Which of the following does not fall under the specified responsibilities of a facilitator?

(A) Gather together the service implementation team
(B) Lead team meetings
(C) Ensure the client is making progress towards specified goals
(D) Guiding discussions in meetings

Question 64

Which of the following is not a common method for a case manager to help establish a successful working relationship between agencies?

(A) The use of quid pro quo arrangements
(B) Develop a memorandum of understanding
(C) Determine the points of contact for services in key agencies
(D) Capitalize on personal relationships the client may have

Question 65

All of the answers below are a common method of evaluating the success or effectiveness of case management for a particular case except:

(A) Extended services survey
(B) Client satisfaction questionnaire
(C) Client outcome measurements
(D) System outcomes

Question 66

Which of these scenarios is it acceptable for there to be no client consent in which a third party can obtain client information?

(A) For the use of payment for health care operations
(B) A new counselor seeking continuity of care
(C) A co-worker asking for an example to compare to another client
(D) All of the above

Question 67

The documentation of the treatment process is essential for all the following reasons except:

(A) Continuity of care when a client moves
(B) Legal documentation for potential lawsuits
(C) Compliance with Federal Regulations
(D) Sharing of information with third parties external to the case to foster future relationships

Question 68

A treatment facility has a policy of documentation retention to keep files for a minimum period of seven years. Which of the following scenarios is a common reason for maintaining files for longer than the minimum timeframe?

(A) For minors
(B) For clients with records of violence
(C) For clients with a recorded relapse
(D) For multiple substance abusers

Question 69

As per 42 CFR part 2, which of the following is not a requirement for content of the disclosure of client information as per a court order?

(A) Disclosure information shall be limited to that which is essential to the objective of the order
(B) Disclosure information should only be provided to those specifically requesting the ordered information
(C) Provide any measures which are necessary to limit the disclosure for the protection of the patient
(D) Provide the information in a manner that is consistent with the public interest

Question 70

Which of the following is not an entity that may hold record keeping and documentation to a specific standard?

(A) Single State authority
(B) Accreditation bodies
(C) Medical services
(D) Insurance companies

Question 71

The statements below are recorded in the screening documentation for a new client. Determine which statement is an example of an A/P progress note.

(A) The client entered showing signs of withdrawal such as excessive sweating and shaking
(B) The client is potentially showing signs of a co-occurring disorder
(C) The client mentioned having alcohol within the last 3 days on 6 different occasions
(D) The client began to become angry when asked about their spouse

Question 72

What is not an essential element when forming a discharge plan?

(A) Referral source
(B) Outcomes of treatment
(C) Condition of client
(D) Exit interview with client

Question 73

All of the following are statements documented from observations during a session with a client. Which statement is most consistent with effective documentation recommendations?

(A) The client was saying very few words whenever asked a question
(B) The client appeared to be shady during time with groups
(C) The client does not appear to have a strong marriage
(D) The client does not appear to have what it takes to succeed at this point

Question 74

Which of the following is not an element of good clinical documentation?

(A) Include the clients name clearly
(B) All entries need to be signed
(C) All entries should be clearly dated
(D) Errors should be removed entirely

Question 75

Of the goals shown below, which is not a part of an effective recovery management?

(A) Stabilize the client's substance abuse
(B) Avoidance of tempting situations
(C) Improved internal health
(D) Re-establishment as a part of the community

Question 76

What action related to recovery management would be a poor decision to maintain sobriety?

(A) Making amends with anyone who was wronged by the client
(B) Establish a better relationship with peers who also use substances
(C) Healthy eating habits and exercise
(D) Avoid social interactions where substances are present

Question 77

According to the Gorski Developmental Model, what is the first step in the stage of stabilization?

(A) Determine the impetus of abuse
(B) The client needs to recognize the issue
(C) The client needs to recover from withdrawal symptoms
(D) The client needs to commit to a path of recovery

Question 78

What stage in Gorski's Developmental Model is associated with the task of repairing any addiction caused social damage?

(A) Early Recovery
(B) Middle Recovery
(C) Late Recovery
(D) Maintenance

Question 79

What are the early signs of a potential relapse that need to be documented if identified?

(A) Changes in daily structures or attitudes
(B) A new-found defensive demeanor
(C) Change in social behavior
(D) Exhibiting lack of judgment

Question 80

A client who suffered from alcohol abuse has shown signs of relapse and you fear the condition may be deteriorating. What is mostly not an effective technique for interrupting the process of the relapse?

(A) Have the client ignore any thoughts of having a drink
(B) Have the client tell someone immediately when they feel in danger of relapse
(C) Encourage socializing in a safe and sober environment
(D) Have the client recall the negative feelings and actions associated with drinking

Question 81

The approach to the recovery process can best be described as:

(A) Primarily reaching abstinence as the goal
(B) A crisis management process
(C) A professionally directed process
(D) A long-term self-growth process

Question 82

Which of the following is not an example of the harm reduction model of recovery?

(A) Designated driver
(B) Drug substitution
(C) Behavior modification
(D) Prolonged periods of abstinence

Question 83

Four clients can be classified by some defining characteristics as determined in their assessment. Which is least likely to benefit from a traditional 12-step program recovery?

(A) Alcohol abuser with severe social anxiety
(B) Alcohol abuser with co-occurring mental disorder
(C) Cocaine abuser with a history of religious involvement
(D) Meth abuser with a fear of isolation

Question 84

Which of the following is not often considered a trigger for a potential relapse?

(A) Negative emotions such as sadness or loneliness
(B) Having a reason to celebrate such as a new job
(C) Sensory stimulants familiar during times of drug use
(D) None of the above

Question 85

What statement below is not consistent with the SAMHSA principles of recovery?

(A) Cultural differences impact recovery
(B) Recovery requires the direction of professional help
(C) Recovery is self-directed
(D) Recovery can be achieved in many ways

Question 86

What is the most accurate estimate of individuals in recovery who sought out or used professional help?

(A) 5%
(B) 25%
(C) 75%
(D) 90%

Question 87

What is not a characteristic of an effective and successful therapeutic alliance?

(A) A strong bond between client and counselor
(B) Collaboration between counselor and third-party entities
(C) Agreement on treatment techniques
(D) Agreement on treatment goals

Question 88

What is an ineffective method for a counselor to develop a strong relationship with a client?

(A) Exhibit a thorough knowledge of expertise in addiction treatment
(B) Use facts to support recommendations
(C) Make connections between the client's experiences and the counselor's clinical knowledge
(D) Explain to the client what to expect from experiences the counselor is familiar with from other clients

Question 89

What action as described below is not consistent with the technique of motivational interviewing?

(A) Summarizing what the client says to show good listening
(B) Ensure an argument is dealt with quickly and sternly
(C) Continue to reinforce agreed upon goals
(D) Make the client aware of actions inconsistent with their goals

Question 90

When counseling a client with a co-occurring disorder, what specific technique is most appropriate to be emphasized?

(A) Using repetition to ensure an understanding of expectations
(B) Identify high risk situations the client may not be aware of
(C) Help the client find a sponsor
(D) Use positive reinforcement such as privileges to reward progress

Question 91

During counseling, a client who has now been abstinent for some significant amount of time and has adjusted to a new lifestyle, has indicated boredom with their current situation. He says his old life was certainly much more exciting. What is not an appropriate technique to avoid a relapse?

(A) Remind the client of the pain from substance abuse
(B) Challenge the client appropriately on the reality of what he remembers as enjoyable times
(C) Suggest new activities that may fill the void
(D) None of the above

Question 92

What is not an effective technique for helping a client utilize a mutual self-help group?

(A) Prescribe the best group for the client
(B) Have exit surveys to evaluate the client's reactions
(C) Provide a briefing on the dynamics of the group
(D) Help to overcome logistical issues

Question 93

What is not consistent with the philosophies of motivational interviewing?

(A) Collaboration
(B) Acceptance
(C) Compassion
(D) Intervene

Question 94

What is mostly not a realistic expectation that should be set from a counselor to prepare the client for sessions?

(A) Confidentiality will be kept
(B) Start times will be enforced
(C) Sessions where the client arrives under the influence will be analyzed for further insight
(D) There may not be any contact outside of the predetermined times

Question 95

What model of substance abuse treatment is consistent with having a philosophy related to the cause of abuse as being a "defect of character"?

(A) Medical Model
(B) Spiritual Model
(C) Sociocultural Model
(D) Psychological Model

Question 96

What is most likely a poor example of self-disclosure during a counseling session?

(A) Telling the client that you observe a certain emotion in today's session
(B) Providing detailed stories to try to connect with the client
(C) Acknowledging a similar interest to build rapport
(D) None of the above

Question 97

What is not an effective example of empathy towards a client?

(A) Express your sincere remorse when the client explains a difficult time
(B) Provide an example of experience with a similar feeling
(C) State the feelings you believe the client is going through
(D) Use active listening to ensure the client knows you understand the story

Question 98

What is not an example of evidence-based therapy?

(A) Pharmacotherapy
(B) Cognitive Behavioral Therapy
(C) Solution Focused Brief Therapy
(D) None of the above

Question 99

Of the following examples of treatment programs, which is considered a long-term method?

(A) Residential treatment
(B) Medication-assisted treatment
(C) Residential therapeutic community treatment
(D) Outpatient counseling

Question 100

When implementing withdrawal management or detoxification, what is not an appropriate expectation of the process?

(A) It will last typically less than ten days
(B) This is an opportunity to evaluate the client's mental state while intoxicated
(C) There is a potential for medical issues and a professional should be present
(D) All of the above

Question 101

A client who is still employed is addicted to opioids and requires treatment. He is also physically disabled which makes it difficult for him to leave the home. His family life while impacted is still supporting and intact. Which of the following treatment options is most likely appropriate?

(A) Outpatient treatment
(B) Halfway house
(C) Therapeutic community
(D) None of the above

Question 102

What is a medication that may have benefits for the treatment of someone with an opioid addiction?

(A) Methadone
(B) Disulfiram
(C) Acamprosate
(D) None of the above

Question 103

What type of group counseling is effective in providing information to the client about substance abuse?

(A) Psychoeducational
(B) Skills development
(C) Support
(D) Interpersonal process

Question 104

Which of the following substances is there no conclusive evidence to support an effectiveness of any medication for abuse treatment?

(A) Alcohol
(B) Tabaco
(C) Methamphetamine
(D) Heroin

Question 105

When determining the presence of a crisis, what statement is true?

(A) A crisis occurs if there is a perceived traumatic event regardless of the mental state of the client
(B) If a traumatic event occurs but the client has a stable mental state there is no crisis
(C) A crisis involves only short-term consequences
(D) A crisis may not include a catalyst

Question 106

What is not a generally an identified step in the process of crisis intervention?

(A) Assess the extent of the crisis
(B) Identify the problem at hand
(C) Determine potential solutions
(D) Establish a relapse strategy

Question 107

What is not an effective strategy for deescalating a crisis situation?

(A) Ask questions about the client's past that may identify the root of the problem
(B) Use verbal de-escalation
(C) Take steps to establish a rapport with the client
(D) Whenever possible, meet with a client in person to deal with a crisis

Question 108

As per general AA teachings, what is not a part of the HALT acronym related to relapse prevention?

(A) Hunger
(B) Anger
(C) Loneliness
(D) Temptation

Question 109

What in contemporary terms is the most prevalent way to describe the goal of relapse prevention?

(A) Have the proper tools necessary to intervene when warning signs arise
(B) Promote healthy and positive changes in one's life to prevent relapse
(C) Prepare the client for the inevitable by having an appropriate plan in place
(D) None of the above

Question 110

What is not consistent with the strategies in relapse prevention therapy?

(A) Identify relapse as a process
(B) Learn to cope with urges and cravings
(C) Learn techniques to minimize damage if a relapse does occur
(D) After a relapse, be prepared to move on completely

Question 111

What is not a category of techniques which can be used for coping as a part of relapse prevention therapy?

(A) Behavioral
(B) Physical
(C) Cognitive
(D) None of the above

Question 112

What is not a primary component of the CENAPS Model of Relapse Prevention?

(A) Assessment
(B) Warning Sign Identification
(C) Warning Sign Management
(D) Relapse Counseling

Question 113

What is the main difference between the Marlatt and Gordon Model of Relapse Prevention and the CENAPS Model?

(A) CENAPS uses abstinence-based treatment
(B) CENAPS encourages lifestyle changes as essential
(C) CENAPS teaches early identification of warnings
(D) All of the above

Question 114

What is not identified as one of the most common triggers for a relapse?

(A) Unpleasant emotions
(B) Interpersonal conflict
(C) Physical pain
(D) Social pressure

Question 115

Evidence based practices and programs have all of the following goals except?

(A) Eliminate unverified practices
(B) Incorporate the opinions of clinical experts
(C) Use science to determine usable evidence
(D) Incorporate the individual tendencies of the client and caregiver into the plan of treatment

Question 116

Management of an agency wants to implement a new evidence-based program into the current framework. What is not necessary for the full integration of the new practice?

(A) Training for counselors on the expectations of the new practice
(B) Client interviewing for the potential of use
(C) Implementation of new policies regarding the program
(D) Evaluation of how the new practice may affect other partners

Question 117

Fidelity of the implementation of evidence-based practices can be disrupted by all of the following except:

(A) Gradual loss over time
(B) Failure to appropriately apply trained techniques
(C) Implementation in different settings
(D) None of the above

Question 118

Which of the following is the basis behind cognitive behavioral therapy?

(A) A user must become abstinent to achieve recovery
(B) Managing a person's thoughts, not their circumstances, affects their internal well-being
(C) Triggers for relapse are avoidable
(D) Employ a plan for traumatic events

Question 119

Which therapeutic approach can be characterized by including battery assessment sessions to incur rapid development?

(A) Motivational enhancement
(B) Contingency management
(C) Cognitive-Behavioral
(D) Trauma

Question 120

Which of the following actions can be classified under a trauma-specific approach?

(A) Explaining the impact of trauma on the mental state of a client
(B) Ensuring the client feels the safety of the space around them
(C) Enrolling a client in a PTSD program
(D) Reassurance of recovery being possible

Question 121

What model of family therapy is most often associated with members of the family not addicted to substances developing a codependence?

(A) Family disease model
(B) Structural model
(C) Cognitive-Behavioral model
(D) Systems model

Question 122

Which of the following is an example of cultural adaptation for the use of evidence-based practices?

(A) Translating questions
(B) Adjusting the progression of steps
(C) Providing an interpreter
(D) None of the above

Question 123

Which of the following is not healthy behavior as it relates to enabling in a relationship?

(A) Trying to repair relationships that may have been affected by the substance abuse
(B) Striving for autonomy in the relationship
(C) Evaluating decisions based on long-term consequences
(D) Not intervening in the consequences of poor decisions related to substance abuse

Question 124

The more traditional measurement of client progress involving tracking the achievement of goals is what type of assessment?

(A) Qualitative
(B) Quantitative
(C) A combination of both qualitative and quantitative
(D) Neither qualitative or quantitative

Question 125

Which of the following statements is not true regarding the connection between substance abuse disorder (SUD) and HIV/AIDS?

(A) Treatment for SUD actually doubles as HIV prevention
(B) Those who have both SUD and HIV/AIDS are subject to higher rates of mental disorders than those with only SUD
(C) Risk reduction is essential for both SUD and HIV
(D) SUD treatment can help prevent the spreading of HIV/AIDS

Question 126

Regarding treatment for substance abuse disorders among individuals with physical disabilities, which of the following statements are true?

(A) They are less likely to seek treatment
(B) They are more likely to seek treatment
(C) There is no difference from the general population in their likelihood to seek treatment
(D) None of the above

Question 127

What is the regulation with the highest precedence for ethical considerations?

(A) Common Sense
(B) Administrative regulations
(C) Contracts
(D) Federal Law

Question 128

What statement below is not consistent with the core principles of trauma-informed care?

(A) Have the client recognize the connection between behaviors and trauma
(B) Establishing a clear, single source of decision making for consistency
(C) Establishing healthy relationships is important to recovery from traumatic events
(D) Instill a feeling of safety

Question 129

As per the Privacy Rule under HIPAA, clients have the right to ask for all of the following except?

(A) A copy of their record
(B) Modifications to the record based on mistakes
(C) Meeting minutes where the client was discussed
(D) Information regarding anyone else who has seen the record

Question 130

What is not an accurate statement regarding women and substance abuse?

(A) When given the opportunity, men are more likely try drugs for the first time
(B) The effects of drugs are physically different for women than for men
(C) For the general population more males than females suffer from substance abuse
(D) Men are more likely to be put in a situation to use drugs for the first time

Question 131

What is not a true statement regarding the fundamentals of professional codes of ethics?

(A) There is now an agreement among professionals of a universally accepted code of ethics
(B) The code of ethics may include vague statements
(C) The code of ethics may not include contemporary ideals
(D) There may be multiple codes of ethics which conflict

Question 132

When counseling a client who is describing some of the events he attended over the weekend, he describes an action that does not quite "feel right" to you. Which of the following elements of morality are you experiencing?

(A) The counselor as a person
(B) Moral sense
(C) Values
(D) None of the above

Question 133

As defined by Corey et al., what is not one of the six guidelines for daily ethical conduct?

(A) Provide informed consent
(B) Ensure client confidentiality
(C) Honor cultural values
(D) None of the above

Question 134

Which of the following is not consistent with proper informed consent?

(A) The client must have a rational capacity to provide consent
(B) The client must show an understanding of what is being consented to
(C) The client must consult with a third party for consent regarding medical issues
(D) The client must feel they are acting voluntarily

Question 135

Which of the following is not an acceptable means of releasing client information as per 42 CFR?

(A) With the client's written consent
(B) Without client consent for reasons specified in the regulations
(C) With a court order
(D) None of the above

Question 136

The Code of Federal Regulations for Confidentiality (42 CFR) is consistent with all of the following statements except:

(A) Regulations for former personnel have different requirements for current personnel
(B) All records whether written or not are covered under unauthorized disclosure
(C) Clients must be provided with a summary of the regulations
(D) Minors must be the ones to provide written consent in regard to their own case

Question 137

Of the elements shown below, what not required on a written consent form?

(A) The receiving organization or individual
(B) A description of the information provided
(C) The client's signature
(D) The date the client was consulted about the release of information

Question 138

What is not considered an acceptable way of maintaining appropriate boundaries with a client?

(A) Avoiding a plutonic relationship with a client outside of treatment
(B) Avoiding any physical contact
(C) Strongly encouraging a 12-step program due to the counselor's own experiences
(D) Avoiding any romantic relationships with the client

Question 139

What is not a stage as a part of cultural competence?

(A) Destructiveness
(B) Blindness
(C) Competence
(D) Rebuilding

Question 140

When counseling a parent on how to have constructive discussions with their child about substance abuse, what is not an example of appropriate advice?

(A) Be calm and patient
(B) Ensure the child knows they are to blame and should take responsibility for their own actions
(C) Use thought provoking questions
(D) Prepare for the encounter with a plan

Question 141

When evaluating cultural considerations for a client, which of the following is an appropriate way to approach the determination of any relevant facts?

(A) Stereotypes can be used as a basis for understanding
(B) Stereotypes can be used as a determination of understanding
(C) Generalizations can be used as a basis for understanding
(D) Generalizations can be used as a determination for understanding

Question 142

What is a defining characteristic of the competence and proficiency stage of cultural competence?

(A) Acknowledging the need for training in cultural competency
(B) Recognizing the need to adopt culturally responsive practices
(C) Implementing culturally responsive practices
(D) Understanding that there are differences between cultural groups

Question 143

What is not an effective method to implement for ensuring cultural sensitivities are practiced?

(A) Using culturally appropriate communication
(B) Integrating traditions or customs of the client into services
(C) Consulting other service providers for best practices
(D) None of the above

Question 144

What is considered the highest period of risk for the use of substances for adolescents?

(A) Entering middle school
(B) Entering high school
(C) The time of onset puberty
(D) None of the above

Question 145

When developing substance abuse prevention programs, which of the following types is designed to target individuals who are already experimenting with substances?

(A) Universal
(B) Selective
(C) Indicated
(D) Individual

Question 146

Which of the following substances is classified as DEA Schedule I?

(A) Rohypnol
(B) Prescription Sedatives
(C) Mescaline
(D) None of the above

Question 147

Which of the following substances does not have enough research to support if behavioral therapies can be used effectively for treatment?

(A) Inhalants
(B) Cocaine
(C) Marijuana
(D) Methamphetamine

Question 148

Which of the following substances does not have any known additional effects when used in combination with alcohol?

(A) Mescaline
(B) Methamphetamines
(C) PCP
(D) Prescription Opioids

Question 149

In comparison to voluntary treatment versus legally mandated treatment, which of the following statements are true?

(A) Voluntary treatment is generally more successful
(B) Voluntary treatment has higher retention rates
(C) Legally mandated individuals often remain in the program for longer
(D) Legally mandated individuals have lower attendance

Question 150

What is considered a long-term effect of the use of Marijuana?

(A) Deterioration of senses
(B) Chronic Bronchitis
(C) Distorted perception
(D) Irregular heartbeat

Question 151

Of the following options listed below, _____ is not one of the consecutive stages of a comprehensive assessment.

(A) Recognition of risk
(B) Comprehensive assessment
(C) Secondary assessment
(D) Process evaluation and outcome determination

Question 152

In general, what is a true statement regarding the identification of a problem for someone at risk of substance abuse?

(A) It is common that a significant event will trigger concern
(B) Habits may remain consistent despite the presence of substance abuse
(C) Action is often taken before full addiction is achieved
(D) None of the above

Question 153

What is not a common example of a sign of substance abuse risk?

(A) Changes in routine or habits
(B) Evidence of frequent medical issues
(C) Change in performance at school or work
(D) None of the above

Question 154

When evaluating a client for drug recognition, you note clear physical signs and responses that differ from normal functioning. Using your knowledge of substances, you infer that the potential drug of choice may be a central nervous system stimulant. Which of the following must be performed to complete the process of drug recognition?

(A) Evaluate any other potential cause of noted physical elements
(B) Interview peers about behavior
(C) Determine the specific substance of abuse
(D) Look for signs self-inflicted harm

Question 155

When gathering information for the use in the assessment process, what is least likely a potential source of information?

(A) Existing information
(B) Individual and peer interviews
(C) Field observations
(D) Testing

Question 156

Which of the following information types should most likely be obtained through interviewing and not from existing data sources?

(A) Current mental state
(B) Medical history
(C) Current employment status
(D) History of mental health

Question 157

Which of the following assessment instruments is not considered a self-report type test?

(A) Adolescent Drinking Index
(B) Adolescent Drinking Inventory
(C) CAGE Questionnaire
(D) Comprehensive Drinker Profile

Question 158

When defining counseling, which of the following is not consistent with its intention?

(A) Identification of a problem
(B) Exploration of a problem
(C) Examinations of a person's thoughts and emotions
(D) Consideration of solutions

Question 159

When providing feedback during counseling, what is not consistent with the appropriate guidelines?

(A) Feedback should be given in a timely manner
(B) Feedback should be general to avoid misinterpretation
(C) Feedback should focus on adjustable aspects of someone's life only
(D) Feedback should not be judgmental

Question 160

Of the substances shown below, _____ is not classified as a central nervous system stimulant

(A) Amphetamines
(B) Cocaine
(C) Marijuana
(D) Caffeine

Question 161

Reflection of feeling is often an effective way to express that the counselor is understanding the client's emotional state. What is not an appropriate way to phrase an expression of reflection?

(A) I see you feel...
(B) You appear to be feeling...
(C) I sense that you feel...
(D) Is what you're saying mean you feel...

Question 162

In accordance with the Johari Window Model for Soliciting and Giving Feedback, what is most often the appropriate "pane" for the use of self-disclosure in counseling?

(A) Open
(B) Hidden
(C) Blind
(D) Unknown

Question 163

What is the primary purpose of interpreting as an effective counseling technique?

(A) To ensure the client you understand their needs
(B) To provide a different perspective the client may not have seen or considered
(C) To help understand the emotions of the client
(D) To evaluate the potential risks for the client

Question 164

What is not an example of an appropriate situation where the counselor should use confrontation?

(A) Having the client recognize a truth that is evident from observation
(B) Actions conflicting with statements made by the client
(C) Confronting the client about their own perception vs. actions
(D) None of the above

Question 165

What is the appropriate classification of blocking behavior for group counseling when a client does not feel they can relate to others who have issues of substance abuse?

(A) Type 1
(B) Type 2
(C) Type 4
(D) Type 5

Question 166

If a family is classified as an "alcoholic family" what is not a general characteristic of this dynamic?

(A) Alcohol is the most important thing in the family
(B) Blame is directed away from the alcohol
(C) Everyone shies away from protecting the alcoholic from consequences resulting in isolation
(D) The family situation is not discussed

Question 167

In general, how often should a treatment plan be reviewed?

(A) Every day
(B) Once every 7-10 days
(C) Once per month
(D) Once every six months

Question 168

Peer pressure can be classified into which of the following types of traumas related to crisis prevention?

(A) Situational
(B) Developmental
(C) Intrapsychic
(D) Existential

Question 169

When dealing with crisis intervention what is not an appropriate action for the resolution of the issue?

(A) Ensure the client takes responsibility for making decisions
(B) Reassure the client that the situation will be ok
(C) Remain calm at all times
(D) Avoid making self-interpretations of the situation

Question 170

Which of the following is not an effective means of dealing with a suicidal client?

(A) Tell the client what good things there are in their life
(B) Have a treatment plan ready
(C) Request they postpone the act
(D) Try to identify the precipitating event

Question 171

What is most often the appropriate reason to issue a referral for a client's specific need?

(A) The counselor or agency does not have the resources to address a client's need
(B) The client suggests additional treatment
(C) The counselor does not see an acceptable amount of progress
(D) None of the above

Question 172

What is the primary indicator of an individual who moves from the second stage of addiction (Abuse) to the final stage (Dependency)?

(A) The behavior of the individual becomes evident
(B) The individual experiences a physical or psychological distress when use is stopped
(C) The individual may begin lying about whereabouts or activities
(D) Use becomes a regular part of daily activities

Question 173

When considering different cultural worldviews, which of the following can be defined as putting a greater emphasis on the wellbeing of the group rather than the individual?

(A) Holistic
(B) Spiritual
(C) Community oriented
(D) None of the above

Question 174

A new client is scheduled to arrive for counseling. From background information you see the client is a woman of Asian-American decent who has difficulty with English. What is not an appropriate means of cultural accommodation for the first meeting with the client?

(A) Ensure any material is in multiple languages
(B) Encourage family involvement to support the client
(C) Research common methods of greeting in the client's culture
(D) Provide a translator

Question 175

A personality disorder which can be characterized as including eccentric behavior such as paranoia, can be classified into which cluster as per the DSM-5?

(A) Cluster A
(B) Cluster B
(C) Cluster C
(D) Personality disorder not otherwise specified

Question 176

Regarding confidentiality laws, which of the following statements is false?

(A) State laws govern over federal laws if they are more strict
(B) Federal laws govern over state laws which are less stringent
(C) Federal laws apply no matter the type of program
(D) None of the above

Question 177

Which of the following conditions must be present for a counselor to contact a parent or guardian without the minor's consent?

(A) The minor is determined incapable of making a rational choice
(B) The situation is life-threatening
(C) The risk may be reduced by contacting the parent or guardian
(D) All of the above

Question 178

What is a typically acceptable time frame for the expiration of consent forms?

(A) One month
(B) One year
(C) Five years
(D) Determined on a case by case basis

Question 179

The concept of "Duty to Warn" applies to which of the following scenarios?

(A) A client indicating that they know of the potential for violence committed by a friend
(B) A client indicating that they will commit violence on a co-worker
(C) A client indicating that they will randomly commit an act of violence
(D) All of the above

Question 180

Which of the following is not a factual statement regarding suicide prevention?

(A) Suicide is most often associated with depression
(B) Men commit suicide more often than women
(C) Women are more likely to attempt suicide
(D) Almost half attempted suicides are successful

Question 181

Regarding alcohol use, which of the following BAC levels is a strong indicator of an alcoholic?

(A) 0.10
(B) 0.20
(C) 0.30
(D) 0.40

Question 182

Which of the following is a true statement regarding the connection between alcohol and sleep?

(A) REM sleep does not occur after heavy drinking
(B) Use of alcohol makes someone sleep less
(C) Small amounts of alcohol will not affect the REM cycle
(D) None of the above

Question 183

If it is determined that a client suffering from co-occurring disorders has a more severe mental disorder and a less severe substance abuse disorder, what level of care quadrant can the client be categorized into?

(A) Category I
(B) Category II
(C) Category III
(D) Category IV

Question 184

HIV can be transmitted through all of the following except _____.

(A) Sneezing or cough
(B) Blood
(C) Breast milk
(D) Semen

Question 185

According to DSM-5 after what time period of being clear of any of the eleven criteria is a person said to be in early remission?

(A) 1 month
(B) 2-3 months
(C) 3-12 months
(D) 1 year

Question 186

Which of the following is not an expected symptom of withdrawal from alcohol?

(A) Hallucinations
(B) Tremors
(C) Increased pupil size
(D) Convulsions

Question 187

Post detoxification, which of the following statements is true regarding a rapid relapse?

(A) The rate of rapid relapse decreases significantly with immediate additional treatment
(B) The rate of rapid relapse does not change with immediate additional treatment
(C) Detoxification decreases the chances of a rapid relapse over unassisted withdrawal
(D) Detoxification has no effect on the chances of a rapid relapse over unassisted withdrawal

Question 188

Alcoholics Anonymous encourages members to complete all of the following tasks except
_____.

(A) Realize that they have the power to overcome substances
(B) Assessment of character defects
(C) Committing to a higher power
(D) None of the above

Question 189

What is not a distinct advantage of individual treatment?

(A) More emphasis on the individuals needs
(B) Cost
(C) Flexible time and schedule
(D) Adapts well to those with personality disorders

Question 190

Which type of peer group provides the person suffering from SUD with a chance to develop a new role in the community?

(A) Positive peer influence
(B) Peer teaching
(C) Peer counseling
(D) Peer participation

Question 191

Cocaine withdrawal can be counteracted with all of the following drugs except _____.

(A) Amantadine
(B) Bromocriptine
(C) Buprenorphine
(D) None of the above

Question 192

Aversive conditioning can best be defined as which of the following?

(A) Enforcing negative rewards for unwanted behavior
(B) Enforcing positive rewards for acceptable behavior
(C) Reassociation of the mental state during triggers
(D) None of the above

Question 193

At what point in the process is the primary counselor generally assigned to a client?

(A) Screening
(B) Intake
(C) Orientation
(D) Assessment

Question 194

What is not generally a task which takes place during the orientation of a client?

(A) Discussion of confidentiality
(B) Presentation of rules and regulations of the program
(C) Present client's rights
(D) All of the above

Question 195

What is most commonly not an intended purpose when using the counseling skill of interpreting?

(A) Helps the client realize a different perspective
(B) It breaks down the defense of the client
(C) It helps clarify the problem
(D) It helps to identify and understand the client's feelings about a particular situation

Question 196

What type of discrepancy is present if a client says, "Sobriety is my number one focus." at one time but then later says "I really just want to drink to be with my friends."?

(A) Contradiction of behavior
(B) Discrepancy in self-perception
(C) Contradictory statements
(D) Difference from normal behavior

Question 197

When dealing with confrontation, if a client accepts it well, what is the most appropriate follow-up response?

(A) Focus on current feelings
(B) Provide empathetic response
(C) Reinforce positive behavior
(D) All of the above

Question 198

If a counselor takes the approach of ensuring they are seen as an expert, what type of leadership style is being employed?

(A) Authoritarian
(B) Democratic
(C) Laissez-Faire
(D) None of the above

Question 199

A negative test result for HIV indicates which of the following?

(A) The person being tested has not been infected
(B) The person being tested was infected too recently and could still have HIV
(C) The person being tested is not able to contract the disease
(D) Both A or B

Question 200

A client who is constantly motivated as needing to be right in any situation can be categorized as what?

(A) Monopolizing client
(B) Self-righteous client
(C) Boring client
(D) Hostile client

Question 201

Which of the following is not a precedent that must be resolved before counseling can begin?

(A) Medical assistance
(B) Proper food and shelter
(C) Self-help support
(D) None of the above

Question 202

A person who is reluctant to stop drinking due to fear of withdrawal symptoms is falling into which of Maslow hierarchy of needs?

(A) Physiological
(B) Safety
(C) Esteem
(D) Self Actualization

Question 203

What is most likely not a reason to begin discussions of the termination stage of the counseling process?

(A) Clear client improvement
(B) Philosophical differences between the client and counselor
(C) Counseling goals have been met
(D) Determination of a client's independence

Question 204

When setting rules initially for counseling sessions, what is not an appropriate way to establish limits?

(A) Limit the length of the session
(B) Limit the amount of sessions
(C) Limit the topics available for discussion
(D) None of the above

Question 205

Of the following demographic groups, which has been reported to have the lowest rate of alcohol use?

(A) Hispanic/Latino
(B) White
(C) African American
(D) Asian American

Question 206

Which of the following is an accurate generalization of the lesbian, gay, and bisexual community as it relates to the use of alcohol and drugs?

(A) LGB community is more likely to use than the general population
(B) LGB community is less likely to use than the general population
(C) LGB community is just as likely to use than the general population

Question 207

When dealing with a client from a rural population, what is not an accurate generalization to consider in regard to their mindset towards counseling?

(A) They are often more resistant to help
(B) They are often more concerned about confidentiality
(C) They express more individuality
(D) They are more likely to express emotions

Question 208

What is an accurate estimation of the percentage of homeless people who also have a substance or mental disorder?

(A) 10%
(B) 40%
(C) 66%
(D) 90%

Question 209

All of the following are examples of client resistance except _____.

(A) Arguing
(B) Interrupting
(C) Ignoring
(D) None of the above

Use the following situational narrative to answer questions 210-212:

A client indicates that they always feel peer pressure when out with friends. He blames them and calls them bad influences implying that others would do the same in his situation.

Question 210

If the counselor responds as "We still need to explore your family dynamics. We're not ready to discuss your friends." What type of client resistance reaction technique is being used?

(A) Simple reflection
(B) Amplified reflection
(C) Shifting focus
(D) Agreement with twist

Question 211

If the counselor responds as "You make a good point, it can be difficult to resist this, but you need to recognize a different perspective." What type of client resistance reaction technique is being used?

(A) Simple reflection
(B) Amplified reflection
(C) Shifting focus
(D) Agreement with twist

Question 212

What type of resistance is the client exhibiting?

(A) Blaming
(B) Challenging
(C) Unwillingness
(D) Hostility

Question 213

What is not an example of an open-ended question related to the use of marijuana by a client?

(A) Are you feeling angry about your smoking?
(B) What emotions did you feel the first time you smoked?
(C) What is your family's feelings about your smoking?
(D) What was your experience the last time you smoked?

Question 214

A client you are treating says "I think smoking has been more detrimental than I realized." What type of statement can this be classified as?

(A) Motivational
(B) Counter-motivational
(C) Self-motivational
(D) None of the above

Question 215

What is not one of the four types of motivational statements as per Miller and Rollnick, 1991?

(A) Cognitive recognition
(B) Effective expression of concern
(C) Process recognition
(D) Direct intention to change

Question 216

What best describes the most common pattern of use for a session of cocaine?

(A) Single sitting over a short period of time
(B) Binges lasting 12-36 hours, consuming all available
(C) Binges of extended periods of time ranging from days to weeks
(D) All of the above

Question 217

Which of the following classifications can be defined as inappropriate use of alcohol which is not deliberate and causes an altered mental, physical, and emotional state?

(A) Alcohol use
(B) Alcohol misuse
(C) Alcohol abuse
(D) Alcohol dependence

Question 218

When evaluating assessment tools, which of the following can be defined as a measure of the test's ability to provide results without error?

(A) Reliability
(B) Validity
(C) Consistency
(D) Repeatability

Question 219

In which of the following scenarios may an adolescent revoke consent?

(A) As determined by specific federal law situations
(B) When agreed upon by client and counselor
(C) When parental permission is granted
(D) At any time

Question 220

What is most often not an indicator that the client is ready to move on from the preparation stage of change to the action stage?

(A) The client's resistance decreases
(B) The client becomes more excitable about the potential for change
(C) The client asks fewer questions about the problem
(D) The client asks more questions about the process of change

Question 221

What is most often not an appropriate motivational strategy for the preparation stage of change?

(A) Raise doubts about substance using patterns
(B) Clarify the client's goals
(C) Have the client publicly announce plans
(D) Explore options for change and treatment

Question 222

When evaluating assessment tools for acceptable validity, which of the following types refer to the test's ability to produce consistent statistical results with a separate measure intended to address the sanity trait?

(A) Content validity
(B) Concurrent validity
(C) Predictive validity
(D) Construct validity

Question 223

Which of the following situations allow a parent or guardian the ability to communicate with a program director without the adolescent as per federal regulations?

(A) The adolescent previously applied for services
(B) There is a reasonable assumption that the adolescent does not have the capacity to rationally decide on consent
(C) There is a substantial threat to life or health present
(D) All of the above

Question 224

If a client is in a group session and uses the phrase "The same thing happened to me but worse. Listen to this!" The client is exhibiting what category of behavior?

(A) Monopolizing client
(B) Self-righteous client
(C) Hostile client
(D) Motivated client

Question 225

During preparation for an intervention, what is not an appropriate item to teach the family and friends who will participate?

(A) Substance abuse is the primary issue
(B) Realize the user will not seek help on their own
(C) Decide who is willing to participate in confrontation
(D) None of the above

Question 226

Which of the following does not most appropriately characterize a person's methods of obtaining substances if they are in a stage of dependency?

(A) Will use any means necessary
(B) Will take some of the substance while dealing
(C) Likely to take severe risks to obtain
(D) Willing to perform criminal acts to obtain

Question 227

Which of the following substances are no longer legally manufactured?

(A) Quaaludes
(B) Minor tranquilizers
(C) Barbiturates
(D) None of the above

Question 228

What substance can not be classified as a narcotic?

(A) Opium
(B) Morphine
(C) Heroin
(D) Cocaine

Question 229

What is a false statement regarding narcotics?

(A) All narcotics are illegal
(B) AIDS is linked to narcotics use
(C) Narcotics can be naturally occurring substances
(D) Narcotics can be synthetic

Question 230

In relation to the rewarding effect of substances, what is not an example of positive reinforcement for the continuation of use?

(A) Peer acceptance
(B) Euphoria
(C) Pain relief
(D) Increased self esteem

Question 231

A client indicates that they first started using substances at a party. During this event, people he did not know were congratulatory and excited when he showed that he could drink a large volume compared to others. What type of social cause of substance abuse is this?

(A) Social learning
(B) Social control
(C) Subculture perspective
(D) Social interaction

Question 232

What statement below regarding individualized treatment is false?

(A) Those in individual treatment do better than those in group
(B) Specific types of individualized treatment are better than others
(C) Individualized treatment is especially effective for those with psychiatric problems
(D) None of the above

Question 233

What type of peer group program can be described as one designed to have peer to peer information sharing?

(A) Positive peer influence
(B) Peer teaching programs
(C) Peer counseling, facilitating, and helping programs
(D) Peer participation program

Question 234

What is not a special consideration that must be accounted for during the assessment of women for substance abuse?

(A) Sexual abuse
(B) Hesitation to use male counselors
(C) Typically, higher self-esteem
(D) Dependency issues

Question 235

When establishing rapport during a verbal assessment, what is not a recommended tactic?

(A) Maintain a physical boundary
(B) Make minimal interruptions
(C) Use both yes/no and open-ended questions
(D) Do not let silence be uncomfortable

Question 236

What should be captured during a verbal assessment?

(A) Story of first use of substance
(B) Story of heaviest use of substance
(C) Current use patterns
(D) All the above

Question 237

When a counselor observes a client's physical appearance, what type of skill is being used?

(A) Physical attending
(B) Psychological attending
(C) Self attending
(D) Responding

Question 238

When a counselor ensures they are sitting facing the client in an open and relaxed way, they are using what type of counseling skill?

(A) Physical attending
(B) Psychological attending
(C) Self attending
(D) Responding

Question 239

If a counselor perceives a client as potentially violent during a session, what is the least appropriate course of action

(A) Immediately stop trying to interpret the client's feelings and focus on listening
(B) Show empathy
(C) Reaffirm commitment to helping
(D) Use appropriate self-disclosure to relate

Question 240

What is not most often an intended purpose when utilizing paraphrasing as a counseling skill?

(A) It exhibits counselor understanding
(B) It allows the client to feel like they are running the session
(C) It helps clarify complicated or confusing thoughts
(D) It can help the client to continue in the right direction

Question 241

A counselor is employing reflection during a session. They constantly use the same phrase of "It appears you feel..." What common error is this counselor using?

(A) Timing
(B) Stereotypical language
(C) Shallow response
(D) Deep response

Question 242

What counselor technique does not help in clarifying the client's thoughts?

(A) Summarizing
(B) Paraphrasing
(C) Reflecting
(D) None of the above

Question 243

When utilizing probing as a counselor technique, what is not an essential component?

(A) Identification
(B) Direction
(C) Open ended question
(D) None of the above

Question 244

What is the least appropriate action for a counselor when setting up a referral?

(A) Check with the client to ensure a follow-up on attendance
(B) Ensure the selected organization can handle the situation
(C) Familiarize the client with the selected organization
(D) Provide contact information for the client

Question 245

A client says they will often just stay in bed and not go to work when they know they have a difficult situation at work. What type of mental defense mechanism is being utilized?

(A) Regression
(B) Intellectualization
(C) Repression
(D) Reaction formation

Question 246

Which of the following best describes the definition of alcoholism?

(A) Occurs if intake is enough to damage physical health
(B) Occurs if intake goes beyond customary dietary use
(C) Occurs if the person will drink against their own will
(D) There is no universal definition of alcoholism

Question 247

What statement is true regarding caffeine and addiction?

(A) Scientists believe caffeine use does not release dopamine and therefore is not addictive
(B) The National Institute on Drug Abuse recognizes caffeine as an addictive substance
(C) Caffeine does not produce withdrawal symptoms and therefore cannot be addictive
(D) None of the above

Question 248

What is not an immediate benefit to quitting smoking (within 1 year)?

(A) Risk of heart attack decreases
(B) Improved circulation
(C) Increase in lung function
(D) Stroke risk reduced to non-smoker level

Question 249

A reduction in the minimum drinking age for a population can be considered which of the following types of prevention interventions?

(A) Universal
(B) Selective
(C) Indicated
(D) None of the above

Question 250

Which of the following techniques is least likely considered a form of motivational interviewing?

(A) Client assessment
(B) Brief interventions
(C) Counseling
(D) Drug informational sessions

Question 251

When discussing the process of recovery, what is the most appropriate statement of advice when managing the client's expectations of the process?

(A) Changes most often will occur suddenly
(B) Change is most often a gradual process
(C) Change randomly occurs as instantaneous or gradual
(D) None of the above

Question 252

What is not considered an effective form of motivational strategy most appropriate for a client in the action stage of change?

(A) Have the client publicly announce any plans to change
(B) Have the client identify new means of positive life style habits
(C) Have the client evaluate their support system
(D) Have the client form strategies to avoid high risk situations

Question 253

What is the least accurate statement describing the assumptions behind motivational interviewing?

(A) Ambivalence towards substance abuse is an atypical reaction
(B) Ambivalence towards substance abuse can be resolved
(C) Ambivalence towards substance abuse is common
(D) Ambivalence towards substance abuse must be overcome to achieve recovery

Question 254

A client says the following statement: "I think I am more concerned about my health than I realized." What type of motivational statement is the client using?

(A) Cognitive recognition
(B) Affective expression of change
(C) A direct intention to change
(D) Optimism of an ability to change

Question 255

Which of the following statements can be considered counter-motivational?

(A) Marijuana makes me a more fun person
(B) I can be sober if I wanted to be
(C) What can I do to change
(D) I didn't realize the type of person I am when under the influence

Question 256

A counselor is trying to elicit self-motivational statements from a client. If the counselor says: "What difficulties have you had in your life related to substance abuse?", the counselor's using which of the following techniques?

(A) Problem recognition
(B) Concern
(C) Intention to change
(D) Optimism

Question 257

A client is currently identified as being in the precontemplation stage of change. You make observations to suggest that they have a fear of losing control of their life and are reluctant to let go of the world they live in involving substances. What category of precontemplation does the client most associate with?

(A) Reluctant
(B) Rebellious
(C) Resigned
(D) Rationalizing

Question 258

A client who has difficulty in situations where they are influenced by others to use substances again needs help in which of the following categories of self-efficacy?

(A) Coping
(B) Treatment behavior
(C) Recovery
(D) Control

Question 259

What is mostly considered a false statement about the assessment of a client for co-occurring disorders?

(A) They should only be assessed using tools given the sensitive nature
(B) Always attempt to involve other parties
(C) If you have inconclusive information involve other parties
(D) Use multiple approaches to assessment if needed

Question 260

A client has not specifically expressed an intent or thoughts of suicide but exhibits extreme distress and has been using substances excessively which includes violent behavior. What level of risk can the client be classified as?

(A) Minimal risk of harm
(B) Low risk of harm
(C) Moderate risk of harm
(D) Serious risk of harm

Question 261

As per the Mini-International Neuropsychiatric interview (M.I.N.I.), what indicator below has the highest applied points for the assessment?

(A) Thought about being better off dead
(B) Wanted to harm oneself
(C) Suicidal thoughts
(D) Developed a suicide plan

Question 262

A client indicates that their depression continues even after 30 days of abstinence. What conclusion can be drawn from the information?

(A) The client likely has a presence of a co-occurring disorder
(B) The client does not have a co-occurring disorder
(C) There is not enough conclusive evidence to make a determination about co-occurring disorder

Question 263

Which of the following Medications for the treatment of opioid addiction has not been formally accepted by the FDA?

(A) Methadone
(B) Buprenorphine
(C) Naltrexone
(D) Naloxone

Question 264

What is not an appropriate requirement when evaluating if a client can be approved to be allowed to take home medication?

(A) Absence of recent substance abuse
(B) Stable home environment
(C) assurance of safe storage of medication
(D) None of the above

Question 265

Which of the following is not a true statement regarding women and substance abuse?

(A) Women have different physical responses to substances than men
(B) Women develop health problems due to substance abuse at lower doses than men
(C) Women develop health problems due to substance abuse over longer period of times than men
(D) Women with substance abuse are more likely than other women to have co-occurring disorders

Question 266

If a patient who has substance abuse problems is using opioids for pain treatment, what is not a valid reason for discontinuing the use of the medication?

(A) The opioids no longer stabilize the patient
(B) The patient is using alcohol
(C) The patient has increased use of the medication
(D) None of the above

Question 267

What is a key defining characteristic of intensive outpatient treatment (IOT) as opposed to traditional methods?

(A) IOT has a minimum of 90 days duration
(B) IOT involves a greater frequency of contact and services
(C) IOT is followed by continuing care
(D) IOT involves specific counseling methods

Question 268

What is not often a constraint specific to a counselor treating clients in jail?

(A) The durations are often too short to be effective
(B) Attendance is often lower
(C) The funding is insufficient
(D) There are often not enough counselors

Question 269

An organization is evaluating its cultural competence at all levels. Which of the following would be classified under an organizational task?

(A) Update the mission statement of the organization
(B) Develop cultural advisory boards
(C) Develop a cultural competence plan
(D) Develop culturally responsive procedures

Question 270

The Short Michigan Alcohol Screening test provides a question of whether or not the participant feels guilty when drinking. This test would provide inconclusive data for which of the following cultures?

(A) African American
(B) Asian American
(C) Arab Muslim
(D) Caucasian

Question 271

Drug cultures can be characterized by all of the following except:

(A) Rules
(B) Dress
(C) Language
(D) None of the above

Question 272

Which of the following prescription drug classes is used to treat anxiety?

(A) Opioids
(B) CNS Depressants
(C) Stimulants
(D) Ritalin

Question 273

Which of the following statements is true regarding the number of deaths resulting from opioid use for the 45-56 age range?

(A) Death from opioids is less than all illegal drugs
(B) Death from opioids is more than all illegal drugs
(C) Death from opioids is about the same as all illegal drugs
(D) There is not enough research to make a determination

Question 274

What can be mostly considered a false statement in regard to the therapeutic alliance between a client and a counselor?

(A) The alliance has just as much influence on success as the chosen treatment method
(B) The alliance needs to be continuously monitored
(C) The effect of the alliance is most prevalent in psychodynamic counseling styles
(D) Practices should be chosen which accentuate the alliance

Question 275

A client indicates that they witnessed an act of terror which involved the loss of life. They have developed night terrors and have trouble sleeping as a result of the incident. What type of trauma is the client experiencing?

(A) Single trauma
(B) Repeated trauma
(C) Sustained trauma
(D) None of the above

Question 276

Which of the following group leader actions does not most likely occur in the working stage of group development?

(A) Help members do more self-exploration
(B) Shift learning from inside to outside of the group
(C) Express feelings of termination
(D) Encourage risk taking in real-world situations

Question 277

What group technique employs using a story or problem stated by a member that others can relate to?

(A) Group commentary
(B) Here and now focus
(C) Role playing
(D) Commonality

Question 278

What is most often not likely a typical reason for a silent client?

(A) The client fears self-disclosure
(B) The client may be trying to control the group
(C) The client may fear losing control
(D) None of the above

Question 279

Of the groups listed below, which is least likely to be at risk for suicide?

(A) Teenage male
(B) Teenage female
(C) Men older than 50
(D) Alcohol dependent people

Question 280

When a client is exposed to a traumatic experience, which of the following is most likely a delayed response?

(A) Denial
(B) Mood swings
(C) Detachment
(D) Denial

Question 281

What statement below is first in the traditional 12-step recovery program?

(A) Humbly ask a higher power to remove our shortcomings
(B) Make a searching and fearless moral inventory of oneself
(C) Admit to being powerless over addiction
(D) Believe a greater power can restore our sanity

Question 282

As treatment for substance abuse disorders evolve, which of the following can mostly be considered an outdated practice?

(A) Labeling clients by their identified problems
(B) Increased focus on client strengths
(C) Solution focused model of recovery
(D) Integration of substance abuse treatment with other disciplines

Question 283

Which of the following withdrawal management programs can be classified as ambulatory?

(A) Intensive outpatient treatment (IOP)
(B) Therapeutic communities (TC)
(C) Halfway House
(D) Medication assisted treatment

Question 284

What type of group counseling is mostly for teaching clients about substance abuse?

(A) Skills development
(B) Psychoeducational
(C) Cognitive-Behavioral
(D) Interpersonal Process

Question 285

If a counselor uses role playing as a teaching method, what type of learning style is being used?

(A) Auditory
(B) Visual
(C) Kinesthetic
(D) All of the above

Question 286

Substance abuse recorded among pregnant women under the age of 18 is:

(A) Higher than those aged 18 or older
(B) Lower than those aged 18 or older
(C) About the same as those aged 18 or older
(D) More research needed

Question 287

What element as listed below is most likely not appropriately included in the screening process documentation?

(A) Referral source
(B) Client strengths
(C) Informed consent
(D) Observations of mental state

Question 288

What is not a statement consistent with the characteristics of Motivational Enhancement Theory (MET)?

(A) It evokes rapid change
(B) It guides the client through a step by step process
(C) It focuses on a change in internal motivation
(D) It is especially successful with alcohol and marijuana disorders

Question 289

Which of the following does not fall within a developed continuum of recovery plan?

(A) Behavioral health resources
(B) Support groups
(C) Self-sufficiency services
(D) None of the above

Question 290

As per Taleff (2010) what is not a specific criterion concerning ethics?

(A) Ethics may be internal or external
(B) Intent is relevant to ethical considerations
(C) Ethics must be impartial
(D) Ethics judge human behavior

Question 291

The varying effect of alcohol on an individual is dependent on all of the following except:

(A) Age
(B) Health status
(C) Family history
(D) None of the above

Question 292

What substance as listed below is not considered a hallucinogen?

(A) Ayahuasca
(B) GHB
(C) DMT
(D) Rohypnol

Question 293

A client maintaining a job is satisfying which of the four dimensions of a recovery-oriented system?

(A) Home
(B) Purpose
(C) Health
(D) Community

Question 294

Recovery capital that falls under personal recovery capital is all of the following except:

(A) Financial assets
(B) Problem solving skills
(C) Shelter
(D) Food

Question 295

Which of the following best describes the primary purpose and goal of the screening process?

(A) Engage the client in a comfortable manner
(B) Establish if there is a need for further assessment based on the likelihood of substance abuse
(C) Determine the appropriate course of action for the client
(D) Provide information on the process of treatment

Question 296

Which of the following drug tests can be used to detect drug use over a period of several months?

(A) Breath
(B) Hair
(C) Saliva
(D) Sweat

Question 297

What is not a use of drug testing during SUD treatment?

(A) Indicator of drug use during initial assessment
(B) Track effectiveness of current treatment plan
(C) To determine the need for immediate medical attention
(D) Indication of a cause for adverse effects from prescribed medication

Question 298

What best describes the characteristics of a client with borderline personality disorder?

(A) A disregard for the rights of others
(B) An inability to form meaningful relationships
(C) A clear pattern of instability of relationships and self-image with associated impulsivity
(D) Severe fluctuations in mood

Question 299

What is not a recommended criterion of documentation for a treatment plan as per ASAM?

(A) Identify individual problems or obstacles
(B) Identify individual strengths, skills, and resources
(C) Treatment progress must be measurable
(D) Avoid specific goals and maintain general concepts

Question 300

When assessing the effectiveness of a referral it is noted that a client had a decrease in criminal activity over a substantial time period. This can be classified as what type of measurement outcome?

(A) Client satisfaction
(B) Client outcome
(C) Service system
(D) Counselor evaluation

Question 301

What substance listed below is generally considered to have a greater relative harmful effect on friends, family and others relative to the user themselves?

(A) Alcohol
(B) Methamphetamines
(C) Cocaine
(D) Cannabis

Question 302

What substance administration method is the fastest for the effects to reach the brain?

(A) Injection
(B) Snorting
(C) Smoking
(D) Ingestion

Question 303

The study of the effects a drug has on an individual and the mechanisms of their action is which of the following?

(A) Pharmacokinetics
(B) Pharmacodynamics
(C) Pharmaceutics
(D) Pharmacoeconomics

Question 304

An individual who regularly uses heroin has become tolerant to the effects and is seeking to find the same high with a different substance. She tries morphine but discovers that she needs a significant amount to obtain the desired effects. What is the user experiencing?

(A) Behavioral tolerance
(B) Reverse tolerance
(C) Acute tolerance
(D) Cross-tolerance

Question 305

A substance abuser admits to not feeling normal without the use of the substance. This is a sign of which of the following?

(A) Physical dependence
(B) Psychological dependence
(C) Tolerance
(D) None of the above

Question 306

For a substance to be considered schedule 5, what is the maximum amount of codeine per 100 ml for a cough preparation?

(A) 100 mg
(B) 150 mg
(C) 200 mg
(D) 500 mg

Question 307

Teenagers are often susceptible to substance abuse since they have not yet developed an ability to make sound judgements or resist impulses. This is often attributed to a lack of development in which part of the brain?

(A) Prefrontal cortex
(B) Basal ganglia
(C) Temporal lobe
(D) Cerebellum

Question 308

What correlation can be drawn between the speed at which a substance reaches the brain and the likelihood of addiction?

(A) The faster a drug reaches the brain, the less addicting the substance will be
(B) The faster a drug reaches the brain the more addicting the substance will be
(C) There is no correlation between speed and addiction
(D) There is only a correlation for specific types of substances

Question 309

What substance effects the serotonin neurotransmitter?

(A) Opioids
(B) Alcohol
(C) Ecstasy
(D) Nicotine

Question 310

What model type of behavior therapy includes changing an associated response from unconditioned to conditioned?

(A) Classical conditioning
(B) Operant conditioning
(C) Social Learning
(D) Positive and negative reinforcement

Question 311

A client is discussing her relationships with friends and indicates her frustration with certain behaviors of theirs. If the client says in relation to her friend: "She only goes on trips so that she can show off to other people. She doesn't even like to travel!", what type of defense mechanism can be identified?

(A) Denial
(B) Displacement
(C) Projection
(D) Rationalization

Question 312

The role within a chemically dependent family which most often will use humor to mask the situation is:

(A) Enabler
(B) Scapegoat
(C) Hero
(D) Mascot

Question 313

What is not one of the four primary modules of Dialectical Behavior Therapy?

(A) Client motivation
(B) Mindfulness
(C) Distress tolerance
(D) Interpersonal effectiveness

Question 314

Which of the following is not a part of the "A-B-C theory" for rational-emotive behavior therapy?

(A) Activating event
(B) Beliefs
(C) Congruence
(D) Emotional and behavioral consequences

Question 315

What is a common misconception related to relapse?

(A) Relapse can often be predicted by clear signs
(B) Relapse is commonly a result of a lack of willpower
(C) Relapse can occur with any type of addiction
(D) Relapse is based on the individual's perception of an event, not the event itself

Question 316

Which of the following is true concerning the primary diagnosis of an individual?

(A) The primary diagnosis is always the substance disorder
(B) The primary diagnosis is always the mental health disorder
(C) The primary diagnosis is whichever disorder diagnosed first
(D) The primary diagnosis includes both the substance and mental health disorders

Question 317

What disorder can be defined by two or more years of depressed moods that occur more often than not but without meeting the criteria for major depressive disorder?

(A) Hypersomnia
(B) Bipolar I
(C) Dysthymia
(D) Agoraphobia

Question 318

What personality disorder is characterized by a pervasive pattern of social inhibition and hypersensitivity to being judged?

(A) Avoidant
(B) Borderline
(C) Dependent
(D) Obsessive-compulsive

Question 319

What is the minimum number of depressive symptoms a client must exhibit to be considered for major depressive disorder?

(A) 3
(B) 5
(C) 8
(D) 10

Question 320

What type of substance administration provides the longest half-life?

(A) Inhalation
(B) Injection
(C) Snorting
(D) Ingestion

Question 321

The ARISE Intervention Method consists of three stages. Stage III only can be achieved by which of the following actions?

(A) The individual agrees to take action towards change
(B) The network members agree to enact consequences for the individual if treatment is not sought out
(C) The network works to motivate the individual toward treatment
(D) The individual accepts a lack of control

Question 322

Which of the following crisis stressors can be categorized as transitional?

(A) Divorce
(B) Hopelessness
(C) Trauma
(D) Depression

Question 323

What is a characteristic of mutual support groups that differentiates it from group therapy?

(A) Crisis is resolved
(B) The group empowers change
(C) Membership is selective
(D) Focus on process

Question 324

What stage of group counseling is associated with the group being effective in achieving goals?

(A) Forming
(B) Norming
(C) Storming
(D) Performing

Question 325

When treating a relapse, what is not a recommended practice for a counselor?

(A) Avoid scare tactics
(B) Provide limited, specific options
(C) Minimize confrontation
(D) Do not label the event as a mistake

Question 326

What is the final step of the twelve for Alcoholics Anonymous?

(A) Make a fearless inventory of the self
(B) Make direct amends
(C) Prayer and meditation to improve contact with God
(D) Carry the message to alcoholics and practice the principals in all affairs

Question 327

A client mentions that an associate at work is to blame for all of her financial troubles and it has led to her current substance issues. If the counselor wants to find out more information by saying "Can you please explain and further elaborate what you mean?", what technique is being used?

(A) Paraphrasing
(B) Clarification
(C) Reflection
(D) Summarization

Question 328

Which of the following can be defined as a projection of feelings or attitudes from the counselor to the client?

(A) Disclosure
(B) Self-disclosure
(C) Transference
(D) Countertransference

Question 329

An LGBT client is beginning to show signs of entertaining the idea of being gay. What sexual identity acceptance level is the client experiencing?

(A) Identity confusion
(B) Identity comparison
(C) Identity tolerance
(D) Identity acceptance

Question 330

Which of the following statements is true if a safety sensitive worker refuses to take a drug test?

(A) The test must be rescheduled within 1 week
(B) The test is treated as if it is positive
(C) The test is treated as if it is negative
(D) The employee may refuse on two separate occasions without consequences

Question 331

What statement is most likely to occur in the advanced phase of recovery?

(A) The client begins to develop independence from the treatment facility
(B) The client acknowledges the need for lifestyle changes
(C) The client verbalizes the struggles with ambivalence
(D) The client begins to recognize triggers

Question 332

What is least likely to be a challenge specific to counseling adolescents?

(A) Low self-esteem
(B) Rebelliousness
(C) Private lifestyle
(D) Pessimistic

Question 333

What is the most reasonable percentage of women with a substance abuse disorder that have been physically or sexually abused?

(A) 10%
(B) 40%
(C) 70%
(D) 95%

Question 334

Which of the following populations are not generally considered especially at risk for contracting HIV/AIDS?

(A) Gay men
(B) Minorities
(C) Gay women
(D) Heterosexual women

Question 335

What statement below is a characteristic of Hepatitis B but not of Hepatitis C?

(A) It can be both acute and chronic
(B) People who recover from the virus develop immunity
(C) It causes liver damage
(D) It is contracted through the blood stream

Question 336

A client who identifies primarily with a single culture can be considered:

(A) Acculturated
(B) Bi-cultured
(C) Culturally immersed
(D) Traditional-interpersonal

Question 337

According to psychoanalytical theory, what structure of the mind is responsible for conscient thought?

(A) Id
(B) Ego
(C) Superego
(D) Antiego

Question 338

Which of the following types of ethics is concerned with a question such as "What are my own core beliefs as a person?"

(A) Principle ethics
(B) Positive ethics
(C) Values ethics
(D) Virtue ethics

Question 339

When faced with an ethical dilemma, what is most likely the first appropriate step to take for decision making?

(A) Implement a course of action
(B) Generate a list of actions
(C) Identify the dilemma
(D) Consult with others

Question 340

What statement is false regarding the ability of an addiction professional to engage in bartering with a client?

(A) There must be a clear written contract prior to services
(B) State and federal laws must allow it
(C) The client must request it
(D) The agreed upon value must be no more than 5 sessions

Question 341

What type of behavior therapy is primarily focused on corrective action related to the fundamental thoughts and behaviors of the client?

(A) Cognitive-behavior therapy
(B) Dialectic behavior therapy
(C) Gestalt therapy
(D) Person-centered therapy

Question 342

What is an acceptable exception to needing consent for a third-party observation of client interaction?

(A) Students in field placement
(B) Direct supervisor of the counselor
(C) Any relative of the client
(D) There are no exceptions

Question 343

According to 42 CFR Part 2. What is not a required element of a written consent to disclose information?

(A) Name of patient
(B) Counselor signature
(C) Expiration date
(D) Name of individual receiving disclosure

Question 344

What can be defined as the continuous practice of self-reflection and self-critique that enables the individual to engage in diverse interpersonal relationships?

(A) Cultural diversity
(B) Cultural competency
(C) Cultural humility
(D) Cultural sensitivity

Question 345

What is not considered a goal of clinical supervision?

(A) Protect the welfare of the client
(B) Empower self-supervision
(C) To monitor performance
(D) To provide personal counseling of the supervisee

Question 346

A supervisor of a counselor begins to acknowledge that the supervisee is beginning to exhibit a level of autonomy in their approach. What level of progression is the counselor most likely in?

(A) 1
(B) 2
(C) 3
(D) 3i

Question 347

What clinical supervision type specifically focuses on the consequences of both the client and supervisee's thoughts and feelings on their interactions, issues and concerns?

(A) Cognitive-behavioral-based supervision
(B) Systematic therapies
(C) Psychodynamic supervision
(D) Feminist model of supervision

Question 348

A counselor suspects that another provider has committed an act which violates ethical conduct. However, there is no evidence of harm resulting from the action. What is the most appropriate course of action?

(A) There is no action needed
(B) Attempt first to resolve the issue informally if feasible
(C) Report the action immediately
(D) Document the action but take no action

Question 349

Vicarious liability of a supervisor includes all of the following except:

(A) Recommending to seek legal advice
(B) Improper advice to a supervisee
(C) Failure to listen fully to a concern
(D) Improper assignment of tasks

Question 350

If a complaint is filed with an ethics board, which of the following is most likely not an appropriate action to take?

(A) Contact the client or individual responsible for the complaint
(B) Only distribute records after seeking legal counsel
(C) Refrain from altering any records
(D) Avoid assuming a lack of harm will have the complaint negated

Question 351

What is not a true statement regarding the requirements for a client to participate in a research study?

(A) No incentives shall be provided in exchange for participation
(B) The client must be informed as to the reason they have been selected
(C) The client must be told the risks and benefits
(D) The specific amount of time commitment must be specified

Question 352

A counselor has a client who also has a child in the same school system. There is no harm that results from the relationship. Which of the following would categorize the situation?

(A) Boundary issue
(B) Boundary violation
(C) Boundary crossing
(D) Boundary indifference

Question 353

Which of the following is not consistent with the role that a Peer Recovery Support Specialist (PRSS) plays in helping the recovery of a client?

(A) The PRSS may provide direction to the client's recovery process
(B) The PRSS must have more recovery experience than the client
(C) The main role of the PRSS is to support and motivate the client
(D) The PRSS may provide access to recovery resources

Question 354

According to SAMSHA TAP 21, which of the following competencies fall under Transdisciplinary Foundation I?

(A) Understand models of addiction
(B) Provide appropriate treatment services based on the individual
(C) Understand diverse cultures
(D) Understand methods for measuring treatment outcomes

Question 355

While understanding every individual is different, what is the most common length of time for a client to reach the maintenance phase of recovery?

(A) 2 months
(B) 6 months
(C) 18 months
(D) 3 years

Question 356

A potential client takes a Drug Abuse Screening Test 20 (DAST-20). Which of the following score ranges would indicate the potential for a severe substance abuse disorder?

(A) 0-5
(B) 6-10
(C) 11-15
(D) 16-20

Question 357

A Discharge Summary and Continuing Care Plan Form should include all of the following elements except:

(A) Discharge reason
(B) Client compliance
(C) Objectives for continuing care
(D) Diagnosis

Question 358

For Person-centered therapy to be effective the counselor must adhere to all of the following attitudes except:

(A) Analysis of resistance
(B) Congruence
(C) Unconditional positive regard
(D) Accurate empathic understanding

Question 359

A client indicates that she has this feeling at parties that she needs to ensure she gets positive approval from everyone she meets. It gives her anxiety about going and when she leaves a party it makes her drink more often. What mental behavior most appropriately describes the client's situation?

(A) Negative reinforcement
(B) Operant conditioning
(C) Codependence
(D) Fictional finalism

Question 360

A client has both a substance abuse disorder and a mental health disorder. The agreed upon plan indicates that treatment for both will occur simultaneously but separate. What type of treatment is being implemented?

(A) Parallel treatment
(B) Sequential treatment
(C) Integrated treatment
(D) Bi-integration treatment

Question 361

After a trigger occurs, the client will enter the first stage of relapse which is:

(A) Emotional relapse
(B) Acute relapse
(C) Mental relapse
(D) Physical relapse

Question 362

When referring the client to a new primary care service, all of the following will help to avoid being charged with abandonment except:

(A) Ensure the client proceeds with the referral despite any willingness to change
(B) Discuss the specific reasoning for termination
(C) Provide termination sessions
(D) Provide an emergency plan for the client

Question 363

A physical condition assessment would fall under which dimension of the American Society of Addiction Medicine (ASAM) Multidimensional Assessment?

(A) Dimension 1: Acute Intoxication and Withdrawal Potential
(B) Dimension 2: Biomedical Conditions and Complications
(C) Dimension 4: Readiness to change
(D) Dimension 6: Recovery/Living Environment

Question 364

What nonverbal response is most likely to not be associated with feelings of anger?

(A) Shaking of head
(B) Lowered, drawn together eyebrows
(C) Open unfolded arms
(D) Tight lips

Question 365

A client begins to make references to suicide and exhibits feelings of hopelessness. What is the next stage in the natural progression in suicide ideation?

(A) Talking about suicide
(B) Devising a plan for suicide
(C) Actions being taken to carry out the plan
(D) Attempting suicide

Question 366

The need statement of an individualized treatment plan will likely include all of the following except:

(A) Examples of difficulties the client is facing
(B) Specific challenges to the client
(C) Goals for the client
(D) Any issues the client has identified

Question 367

At what time interval should progress notes be developed and filed?

(A) For each interaction with the client
(B) For only agreed upon interactions with the client
(C) On a monthly basis
(D) For notable interactions or instances

Question 368

Which of the following would not be considered as a part of a multidisciplinary addiction treatment team?

(A) Pharmacist
(B) Family Therapist
(C) Peer Recovery Support Specialists
(D) None of the above

Question 369

According to the Stokes and Tate model of group therapy stages, which stage is mainly characterized by the group experiencing conflict?

(A) Acquaintance stage
(B) Groundwork stage
(C) Working substage
(D) Closing substage

Question 370

What question or statement below would be classified as an action response?

(A) How does your brother's dealing of substances make you feel?
(B) I think it is clear you are feeling angry right now
(C) I believe you are saying you feel a lack of control at home. Is this correct?
(D) As I see it you are afraid to contact your brother, would you agree?

Question 371

A counselor is considering sharing a personal story to a client. What is the least appropriate means of evaluating if the counselor should self-disclose the information?

(A) The story may increase the connection with the client
(B) The story is uncomfortable for the counselor to share but may benefit the client
(C) The story may cause the client to have a revelation about themselves
(D) The client will likely see this as helpful

Question 372

Which of the following is an example of a conditioned response?

(A) Providing praise after a period of abstinence
(B) Reassociation of alcohol with positive feelings to nausea
(C) Understanding how a trigger is associated with substance use
(D) Providing punishment for undesirable behavior

Question 373

Which of the following tests is most appropriate for the assessment process and not the screening process?

(A) Michigan Alcoholism Screening Test (MAST)
(B) Addiction Severity Index (ASI)
(C) Alcohol Use Disorders Test (AUDIT)
(D) Cut down, annoyed, guilty, eye-opener (CAGE)

Question 374

A safety-sensitive transportation employee has never had a positive result for a drug test. Which of the following testing scenarios is not appropriate?

(A) Pre-employment
(B) Reasonable cause
(C) Follow-up
(D) Random

Question 375

Which of the following emphasizes self-actualization, freedom of choice and critical thinking as a basis for moral decision making?

(A) Humanistic ethics
(B) Clinical pragmatism
(C) Situational ethics
(D) Religious ethics

Question 376

Which of the following programs allows the client the ability to remain in their primary residence with structured treatment sessions?

(A) Detoxification treatment
(B) Inpatient treatment
(C) Residential treatment
(D) Intensive outpatient

Question 377

A type of substance that prevents other neuro transmitters from binding to a neuron thus blocking activation is which of the following?

(A) Agonist
(B) Antagonist
(C) Partial agonist-antagonist
(D) Glutamate

Question 378

How many fluid ounces of wine is the U.S. standard drink equivalent?

(A) 4
(B) 5
(C) 7
(D) 8

Question 379

What statement is most often true regarding caloric intake from food for people with an alcoholic substance abuse disorder?

(A) The caloric intake from food is more for those with a SUD
(B) The caloric intake from food is less for those with a SUD
(C) The caloric intake from food is not affected for those with a SUD
(D) There is no correlation between caloric intake from food and those with a SUD

Question 380

What medication when used to treat alcoholism causes the user to become physically ill if they consume alcohol while the substance is in the body?

(A) Disulfiram
(B) Naltrexone
(C) Acamprosate
(D) Methadone

Question 381

Which of the following is an opioid but not an opiate?

(A) Morphine
(B) Codeine
(C) Thebaine
(D) Hydrocodone

Question 382

Which of the following substances does not mostly past through in the liver?

(A) Opioids
(B) Inhalants
(C) Barbiturates
(D) Cocaine

Question 383

What substance below is not classified as an anesthetic?

(A) Ether
(B) Chloroform
(C) Nitrous oxide
(D) Butane

Question 384

What is not a method in which inhalants may be administered into the body?

(A) Sniffing
(B) Injecting
(C) Bagging
(D) Vaporizing

Question 385

What is the most common method for adolescents who abuse opioids to obtain the substance?

(A) Received from friends or family
(B) Prescribed through doctor
(C) Theft
(D) Sought out illegal dealer

Question 386

The compression of cannabis resins into concentrate creates which of the following?

(A) Hashish
(B) Kief
(C) Shatter
(D) BHO

Question 387

An adult client is describing her patterns of alcohol use. Which of the following scenarios would classify as binge drinking (all drinks standard US size)?

(A) 1 glass of wine everyday over a week
(B) 8 glasses of wine over two days
(C) 6 glasses of wine over a 12-hour period
(D) 4 glasses of wine over a 2-hour period

Question 388

What product below does not contain caffeine?

(A) Yerba mate
(B) Cheroot
(C) Yoco
(D) Guarana

Question 389

Which of the following is not a shared characteristic between crack and cocaine?

(A) Contains coca
(B) Can lead to an overdose
(C) The effect is instantaneous
(D) Classified as a stimulant

Question 390

All of the following are exceptions to privileged communication except:

(A) Court ordered exam
(B) Harm of others
(C) Established dual relationship
(D) Abuse of others

Question 391

A counselor is reviewing results from a specific assessment instrument. She notices that there is a difference often in the intended goal of the evaluation and the results. The assessment likely has a low_____.

(A) Usability
(B) Reliability
(C) Validity
(D) Content Validity

Question 392

If a client and counselor engage in technology assisted counseling (TAC), what is not an associated disclosure?

(A) The client is not protected under certain state or federal laws
(B) The connection is not secure
(C) Possibility of technological failure
(D) Emergency procedures

Question 393

When preparing to screen an adolescent for the use of alcohol, what is not a recommended practice to help encourage honest participation?

(A) Provide alone time
(B) Reassure that adolescent drinking is normal
(C) Fully explain confidentiality rules
(D) Reassure them they are not in trouble

Question 394

Which of the following activities related to alcohol abuse has the highest estimated economic impact?

(A) Crashes, fires, and other damage
(B) Lost earnings due to alcohol-related illness
(C) Lost earnings due to premature death
(D) Medical consequences

Question 395

At what level of exposure are the risks of second hand smoke at a tolerable level?

(A) Less than once per week
(B) A distance of no less than 20 ft
(C) A distance of no less than 50 ft
(D) There is no risk-free level of exposure

Question 396

What is not a key component to administering motivational incentives?

(A) Identify desired behavior
(B) Evaluate frequency of distribution
(C) Ensure an expression of empathy
(D) Evaluate the right choice of incentive

Question 397

What statement below is true regarding smokeless tobacco products?

(A) Does not cause cancer
(B) Contains less harmful chemicals than cigarettes
(C) Is not addictive
(D) Is recommended as an aid to slowly quit cigarettes

Question 398

A client with a substance abuse disorder has also been diagnosed with having depression. What behavior is least likely to be typical with this type of client?

(A) Quick to come to conclusions
(B) Unquestioning belief in others opinions
(C) Discounting positives
(D) Extremist world view

Question 399

An adolescent of age 10 has been screened and has indicated that there was an incident in which he had alcohol with friends. At what level of risk is most appropriate for the client?

(A) None
(B) Low
(C) Moderate
(D) High

Question 400

According to SAMSHA TAP 21, what practice dimension includes competency 48: Reassess the treatment plan at regular intervals?

(A) I
(B) II
(C) IV
(D) VI

Question 401

Which of the following characteristics is more representative of sympathy rather than empathy?

(A) Awareness of others experiences
(B) A more automatic or effortless action
(C) More concern for understanding rather than alleviating pain
(D) Sharing feeling with the client

Question 402

A client with substance abuse is also suffering from depression. Which of the following is not a true statement regarding the use of antidepressants?

(A) Effects can be expected after 4-6 weeks
(B) If one type doesn't work, another can be tried
(C) Antidepressants have a high risk of abuse
(D) There is no predictor of the best type of medicine

Question 403

Which of the following non-opioid analgesics is addictive?

(A) Anticonvulsants
(B) Muscle relaxants
(C) NSAIDs
(D) Acetaminophen

Question 404

What stage of pregnancy has research confirmed it is safe to consume small amounts of alcohol?

(A) None
(B) 1st trimester
(C) 2nd trimester
(D) 3rd trimester

Question 405

What hallucinogenic substance is often consumed by means of brewing into a tea?

(A) Peyote
(B) Ketamine
(C) LSD
(D) PCP

Question 406

A pregnant woman seeking treatment indicates that she did not proceed due to the lack of groups specifically for women who are or have been pregnant. What type of obstacle is preventing her from seeking treatment?

(A) Sociocultural
(B) Interpersonal
(C) Intrapersonal
(D) Structural

Question 407

What is a research-based fact for PTSD in women as opposed to men?

(A) PTSD is more common in women and has a longer duration
(B) PTSD is less common in women and has a longer duration
(C) PTSD is more common in women and has a shorter duration
(D) PTSD is less common in women and has a shorter duration

Question 408

A parent has a child whom they fear may be experimenting with substances. What is most likely not a reasonable form of advice to help enforce positive parental supervision?

(A) Have some non-negotiable rules
(B) Communicate regularly
(C) Avoid checking in regularly
(D) Have consistency in rule application

Question 409

What is a false statement regarding an overdose from the use of cocaine?

(A) There is medication available to relieve symptoms
(B) Overdose can often cause heart attacks
(C) Overdose can cause seizures
(D) Overdose can cause stroke

Question 410

What statement regarding driving under the influence of substances is false?

(A) Men are more likely than women to drive under the influence
(B) Teenagers are more likely than adults to drive under the influence
(C) More people drive under the influence of alcohol than all other drugs combined
(D) Drunk drivers are most likely to be caught within the first five attempts

Question 411

What is not an FDA approved method for quitting smoking?

(A) Nicotine gum
(B) E-cigarettes
(C) Prescription cessation medicines
(D) Skin patches

Question 412

What therapy type is most effective as a means for establishing rapport in the early stages of treatment with a client?

(A) Client-centered
(B) Existential
(C) Group
(D) Behavior

Question 413

A client in the precontemplation stage has indicated a feeling of hopelessness to change and just feels tired thinking about the effort it would take to make a dramatic shift away from the current lifestyle. What classification best describes the client?

(A) Resigned precontemplation
(B) Rationalizing precontemplation
(C) Reluctant precontemplation
(D) Rebellious precontemplation

Question 414

At what number of drinks per week is there a significant jump in a male's risk for cirrhosis of the liver?

(A) 5
(B) 14
(C) 20
(D) 32

Question 415

A client is unwilling to accept the extent of the goals a counselor is suggesting. She is willing to give up cocaine but does not see the harm relinquishing marijuana use. If the counselor agrees this is what type of goal resolution?

(A) Giving up
(B) Negotiation
(C) Approximation
(D) Referral

Question 416

What proof is the standard drink for a 1.5 ounce serving of hard liquor?

(A) 40
(B) 60
(C) 80
(D) 100

Question 417

What type of therapy model has been found to be effective specifically for users of stimulants?

(A) The matrix model
(B) Family behavior
(C) Community reinforcement
(D) Cognitive-behavioral

Question 418

What is the most reasonable estimate for the percentage of people with some level of substance abuse disorder that actually receive treatment?

(A) 10%
(B) 40%
(C) 75%
(D) 90%

Question 419

What statement about Fentanyl is false?

(A) It is significantly more potent than morphine
(B) It is only obtained illegally
(C) It relives chronic pain
(D) Can cause an overdose

Question 420

What is not a characteristic of brief therapy?

(A) Less but more intense sessions
(B) Focus on progress not a defined goal
(C) Helpful for a large number of clients
(D) Works with greater client commitment

Question 421

A client with substance abuse disorder decides to attend an acupuncturist for chronic pain management. The client indicates that the acupuncturist is recommending certain herbs and medicines for to go along with the pain. What is the most appropriate response below?

(A) Forbid the client from taking any medication that is not specifically prescribed from the network of care
(B) Allow the client to continue without any action
(C) Document the interaction and take no additional action
(D) Have the client indicate any medication that is being taken for evaluation in the treatment plan

Question 422

Of the substances listed below, which is least likely to cause physical dependence due to common use patterns?

(A) Hallucinogens
(B) Cannabis
(C) Opioids
(D) Caffeine

Question 423

What is a true statement regarding those who are forced to be in rehab vs. those who willingly decide to participate?

(A) There is no significant difference in success rates
(B) Those who are forced in have a higher success rate
(C) Those who willingly participate have a higher success rate
(D) Only women who voluntarily enter treatment have a higher success rate. This is not true for males

Question 424

Of the substances listed below, which is classified as a non-controlled substance?

(A) Amoxicillin
(B) Oxycodone
(C) Testosterone
(D) Methadone

Question 425

A counselor has a high intensity client that has suffered a variety of traumas. The counselor has often had constant emotional reactions to the suffering experienced by this client and is exhausted from the intensity of the required empathy. If the counselor begins to experience a lack of focus and emotional stability elsewhere, what condition is being suffered?

(A) Dual relationship
(B) Professional impairment
(C) Value conflict
(D) Compassion fatigue

Question 426

What is least likely to be considered a gateway drug?

(A) Alcohol
(B) Steroids
(C) Marijuana
(D) Tobacco

Question 427

What type of drug test produces rapid results by using antibodies to detect the presence of substances?

(A) Thin layer chromatography
(B) Immunoassay test
(C) Gas chromatography
(D) Hair analysis

Question 428

What hallucinogenic substance has a currently accepted medical use?

(A) LSD
(B) Salvia
(C) Ketamine
(D) Peyote

Question 429

What substance listed below can cause a reverse tolerance?

(A) Amphetamines
(B) Stimulants
(C) Nicotine
(D) Hallucinogens

Question 430

A client who wishes to seek treatment has an established co-occurring disorder of substance abuse and mental disorder. The facility at which she applies does not have the specific necessary services to treat the mental disorder but can adequately address the substance abuse. What is the most appropriate ethical decision?

(A) Admit the client
(B) Deny the client
(C) Deny the client but ensure proper referral
(D) Admit the client but only perform an assessment

Question 431

What is not a common means of concealing substances or their use?

(A) Writing utensils
(B) Apples
(C) Books
(D) None of the above

Question 432

Research has linked the heavy use of marijuana for teens with all of the following except?

(A) Lower self esteem
(B) Less likely to graduate
(C) Greater chance of chronic pain
(D) Drop in IQ

Question 433

What is the most appropriate percentage of first-time marijuana users who are aged 12-20 years old?

(A) 20%
(B) 50%
(C) 75%
(D) 95%

Question 434

Without "good cause" a HIPAA complaint should be filed no later than how many days after the subject incident?

(A) 30
(B) 90
(C) 120
(D) 180

Question 435

An incarcerated individual who is receiving treatment for substance abuse disorder is planned to be released soon. What support program is most likely applicable to complete the continuity of care upon release?

(A) Group therapy
(B) Transitional housing
(C) Detoxification
(D) Outpatient treatment

Question 436

A counselor engaging in family therapy has reached the point where they are able to assess and address the feelings of family members of the client with substance abuse disorder. What level of family counselor involvement is the counselor in?

(A) 1
(B) 2
(C) 3
(D) 4

Question 437

An individual can be diagnosed with schizophrenia by exhibiting 2 or more of each of the following characteristics over a month time frame except:

(A) Delusional
(B) Restlessness
(C) Hallucinations
(D) Gross disorganization

Question 438

What is most likely not a recommended strategy to increase retention in treatment?

(A) Rigid treatment schedule
(B) Motivational interviewing
(C) Increased early frequency
(D) Using additional services upfront

Question 439

Which of the following drug paraphernalia is not often associated with marijuana?

(A) Dabbing tool
(B) Cotton balls
(C) Grinder
(D) Scales

Question 440

Dextromethorphan (DXM) is most commonly found in which of the following substances?

(A) OTC Cough suppressants
(B) Peyote cactus
(C) Nutmeg
(D) Air fresheners

Question 441

What culture is often associated with embracing silence instead of attributing it to awkwardness or inefficiency?

(A) White
(B) Latino
(C) African American
(D) Native American

Question 442

What ASAM Criteria level is least appropriate for the use of brief interventions?

(A) 0.5
(B) 1
(C) 2
(D) 3

Question 443

The chemical compound that is more prevalent in dark liquors and is a contributor to hangovers is called _____.

(A) Endorphins
(B) Congeners
(C) Ethanol
(D) Nabilone

Question 444

A counselor is beginning to document a client's conduct that includes repeated instances of drug seeking behavior resulting in using substances after a year of abstinence. Which of the following best defines this type of behavior?

(A) Relapse
(B) Recidivism
(C) Post-acute withdrawal
(D) Reduced tolerance

Question 445

What is the most reasonable estimate for the success rate of antidepressants?

(A) 5-10%
(B) 20-30%
(C) 40-60%
(D) 85-95%

Question 446

Which of the following statements are true regarding adolescents and the what classifies a session as binge drinking?

(A) The amount of drinks for adolescents is the same as adults for binge drinking
(B) The amount of drinks for adolescent girls and boys are the same for binge drinking
(C) The amount of drinks for adolescent boys increases with age for binge drinking
(D) The amount of drinks for adolescent girls increases with age for binge drinking

Question 447

A client is having difficulty with group therapy. When asked about the experience he indicates a difficulty to concentrate and is always being told to stop talking to others during sessions. He also mentioned the difficulty in staying focused during the longer 3-hour sessions. What is the most likely cause of the difficulties as described?

(A) AD/HD
(B) Anxiety disorder
(C) Antisocial personality disorder
(D) HIV

Question 448

After alcohol what is the second most common substance detected at crashes where individuals were driving under the influence?

(A) Marijuana
(B) Cocaine
(C) Heroine
(D) Opioids

Question 449

A client is explaining her group of friends with whom she does hallucinogens. The client says "We like to expand our minds, to be free thinkers, and be creative artistically. We don't think there is anything harmful in the types of drugs we take unlike the heavy stuff. We accept anyone who is tired of the classic perception of taking psychedelics." From the statement the counselor can infer that the drug culture is based on all of the following except:

(A) Age
(B) Gender
(C) Drug type
(D) Common interests

Question 450

A counselor learns that a client is an undocumented worker. The client is very reluctant to share any information personal or otherwise. What most likely is a helpful point of emphasis for this particular client?

(A) Reassurance of confidentiality
(B) Co-occurring assessment
(C) Family dynamics
(D) Basic needs

Solution 1

There are many factors which may lead to addiction and they will vary for each individual. However, we can isolate and identify certain tendencies based on the variables of each case. In this situation, the subject is an adolescent. At this age the influence of peers can have the greatest impact on a person's behavior. This is when a person will begin to break away from the influence of the family which tends to have a larger impact during childhood. Genetics always play a large role in the susceptibility to addiction but since there is no family history, it is difficult to point to the extent of the influence it has in this case. Television and other media while can be somewhat influential, is most often only a minor factor in addiction tendency.

The answer is **(C)**

Solution 2

Models are an attempt to explain simply why people become addicted. Each model theorizes a different main factor in the causation of addiction. The moral model holds humans accountable for their own actions and states that addiction can be controlled by choice of the individual. Addiction therefore is a weakness and is not caused by any genetic or outside influence. The genetic model is the belief that a person's biological makeup is responsible for addiction tendencies. There is also the disease and cultural model which as it sounds sees addiction as a disease. The blended model is an approach that incorporates all potential factors. While family influence can be an influence on a person's addiction, there is no familial model for causation.

The answer is **(D)**

Solution 3

As an individual continues the use of addictive drugs, the chemical effects of the drug begin to take over and the effect of other influences begins to decrease.

The answer is **(C)**

Solution 4

Due its wide availability and being legal, alcohol is the most widely abused substance in The United States.

The answer is **(B)**

Solution 5

There are significant gender differences in relation to the abuse of alcohol. Men in general will tend to drink more in terms of volume and are even more likely to drink alcohol in general. However, alcohol is absorbed differently in women than in men. Despite drinking the same volume, a woman will have more alcohol in their bloodstream and therefore are more likely to have problems of abuse to occur. This also has a greater effect on the health of the individual leading women to have a greater risk of internal damage. Therefore, all the statements are correct.

The answer is **(D)**

Solution 6

While the amount of people addicted to marijuana is very low compared to other substances, it is a common misconception that cannabis is not addictive.

The answer is **(A)**

Solution 7

Since they can be obtained legally and have an appropriate purpose, it may be difficult to determine when prescription drugs are being abused. There are three scenarios in which they are being used improperly:

1. Medication being used by someone other than the intended user
2. Taking the drug in a higher dose or in a different way than it is prescribed
3. Taking a drug for a use other than that which was intended

From the scenarios described above, each one violates one of the abuse rules outlined above.

Therefore, none of the statements are appropriate prescription drug abuse.

The answer is **(D)**

Solution 8

To get someone to commit to treatment they need to recognize the problem internally. Self-motivation to get help is frequently the most common reason identified when someone seeks help. This motivation can however be fleeting and must be acted upon as soon as possible to avoid slipping back into the substance abuse.

The answer is **(A)**

Solution 9

During the initial interview a client can be in a difficult state of mind and establishing a rapport and trust is essential. It is also important to observe and be aware of the person's condition so that you may better assess. Observing their appearance is important so that you can get a sense of the person's self-image.

People who are substance abusers also may have performed unacceptable or even illegal acts, but they must feel as though they are accepted despite your own internal disapproval. This is the only way they will proceed on a path of seeking help.

The use of open-ended questions can be a very useful tool to encourage discussions and more in-depth thoughts. Using yes or no only questions can hinder the progress.

Providing reassurance when appropriate can be useful, but you must be careful as to not over promise that something can be resolved. Giving false hope can lead to mistrust and sever a relationship. Therefore, only provide reassurance when it can be realistically achieved

The answer is **(B)**

Solution 10

Active listening in general is providing reassurance to the client that you understand what is being said and how the client is feeling. There are four specific skills of active listening: Reflecting, Clarifying, Focusing, and Summarizing.

Restating specific words is the use of reflecting a client's conversation. It shows that you can mirror back what was said and that you are indeed listening.

Refocusing appropriately falls under focusing. The client must stay on track and it is your job to keep it so.

Identifying key feelings and thoughts the client has had summarizes the conversation in a way that simplifies things for them and ensures you are getting to the core of their concerns.

Providing stories to relate can be a good way to establish rapport and a connection but it is not a part of active listening. You do not want to take focus away from the client despite your ability to relate to them.

The answer is **(C)**

Solution 11

Screening is an initial evaluation of a client. Screening can identify that a problem exists, confirm suspicions of a problem, or identify that further evaluation is necessary. There are also situations in which it is already established that there is a problem and the screening may be used to measure how severe a problem is. Screening does not go further than this however and the solution to an identified problem should be pushed to the assessment of the client.

The answer is **(B)**

Solution 12

The screening process should adhere to certain appropriate guidelines:

- Screenings should be done in multiple settings and by multiple people
- Information should be gathered from more than one source
- Initial screenings should be brief

While it is important to understand the client as best as possible, the screening stage is not for the in-depth evaluation.

The answer is **(C)**

Solution 13

The MMS is used for co-occurring disorders. The other options are for standard initial screenings.

The answer is **(A)**

Solution 14

While several withdrawal symptoms are quite common among many drugs, the common link is almost always Dysphoria. This is due to the unnatural stimulation of dopamine in the brain that drugs produce causing the user to have a fabricated sense of happiness. As drug use continues, the natural production of this drug becomes altered and stopping use of the substance will cause the subject to have severe feelings of sadness and depression.

The answer is **(C)**

Solution 15

The eight stages of effect for alcohol as per the Catholic University of America are: Sobriety, Euphoria, Excitement 1, Excitement 2, Confusion, Stupor, Coma, and Death. Depression is not one of the stages.

The answer is **(C)**

Solution 16

The defining symptom here is the violent behavior and mood swings. This is very often a result of steroid withdrawals.

The answer is **(D)**

Solution 17

The key factor in this question is the client's current situation and pending legal action. Often when custody is a concern, the court may respond most favorably to a standardized format of questions to rule out as many variables as possible. Therefore, the standardized option is the most appropriate.

The answer is **(A)**

Solution 18

Self-administered tests are a good means of assessment for people who may have trouble speaking or feel shy in interviews. The tests are required to be provided in a low level of reading to accommodate all education levels.

The tests can also be scored providing a quantifiable way to measure the subject

Because they do not require interaction, they can often be administered by less skilled staff.

The answer is **(D)**

Solution 19

When completing an assessment on a non-English speaking person, the choice of translator must be made carefully so that there is nothing lost in communication, confidentiality is maintained, or that there are no biases. Therefore, if your company does not have staff proficient enough in a particular language, an independent one must be used.

The answer is **(C)**

Solution 20

It is very important to note that the first priority must be the health and safety of the client and those around the client before any treatment can begin. If a client enters showing harmful or unhealthy behavior, you must seek medical treatment for them immediately.

The answer is **(C)**

Solution 21

Suicide risk can be assessed based on the guidelines provided by the American Psychiatric Association which provides three domains for assessment: Current presentation of suicidality, history, and risk management.

Alcohol is very often a factor in suicide cases. It is present in almost a third of all suicide cases.

Clients with a family history of suicide are indeed more likely to pose a risk.

Aggression towards others is most often a sign of internal struggle and can be an indicator of a risk of harming one's self

The answer is **(D)**

Solution 22

Hair has the advantage of being able to detect drug use over a long period of time. It can register a use up to several months prior to the test. However, it does not indicate at which specific time the use occurred within that time frame. Therefore, it is not typically used for regular compliance checks.

The answer is **(A)**

Solution 23

Alcohol only stays in the body for a short period of time relative to other drugs. Alcohol leaves the body within a few hours after ingestion.

The answer is **(A)**

Solution 24

Doxylamine is often found in sleep aids and has been linked to false positives for opiates and PCP.

Poppy seeds in high amounts do contain enough morphine to trigger a false test.

Sertraline is an antidepressant which can trigger a test for LSD.

Sesame seeds have no connection to false positives.

The answer is **(C)**

Solution 25

Most often, addiction counselors do not actually officially diagnose the mental health disorder of the client. The assessment can certainly identify the potential presence of the disorder and how it may be affecting the client related to substance abuse, but most often a separate professional will make this call.

The answer is **(C)**

Solution 26

Studies do show that for many people who have mental health issues, the sensitivity to the drugs is actually worse than those without and therefore are more sensitive.

The answer is **(A)**

Solution 27

The DSM-5 recognizes that people's inherent ability to begin substance abuse is not equal and that some people are more susceptible than others. It is important to understand the condition of each individual.

The DSM-5 also categorizes disorders as substance use or substance induced. The induced disorders are mostly a direct result of taking the drugs and are not as a result of a preexisting condition such as a mental disorder.

The answer is **(C)**

Solution 28

Depression as a result of drug use falls under substance induced disorders and is not a substance use disorder.

The answer is **(D)**

Solution 29

The following is the severity scale for SUD:

< 2 not enough information to receive a SUD diagnosis
2-3 Mild disorder
4-5 Moderate disorder
> 6 Severe disorder

The answer is **(C)**

Solution 30

An easy way to remember a generally what to expect from withdrawal symptoms is that the effect of the drug will have the opposite effect during withdrawal. Substances that are classified as depressants will have withdrawal symptoms that are elevated activity such as increased heart rate and shaking. The opposite is also true with stimulants as they will cause restlessness or even insomnia. For this question the depressant alcohol will cause the opposite effect of the other substances listed.

The answer is **(B)**

Solution 31

Almost all withdrawal symptoms will begin to go away over time. There are certain substances however which can cause long-term damage. These include alcohol, some inhalants and amphetamines.

The answer is **(A)**

Solution 32

The intake process is mainly the act of processing the client into treatment. It involves logging information and asking any relevant information that is necessary. It is somewhat an extension of the screening process and is not a part of the treatment process.

The answer is **(A)**

Solution 33

The intake process should establish the following:

- Determine if the client needs treatment
- Perform basic data collection
- Determine any barriers or assets for the clients
- Determine a treatment plan

The answer is **(D)**

Solution 34

The client has the right to have what he or she says be confidential. There are exceptions. One of which is to have information released by the written consent of the client. If the client is alive and of sound mind, they cannot have someone else sign for them.

The answer is **(A)**

Solution 35

A client entering treatment does have a number or required rights which must not be infringed upon. They include:

- Right to Individual Dignity
- Right to Confidentiality
- Right to Non-Discriminatory Services
- Right to Quality Service
- Right to Communication
- Right to Personal Effects
- Right of Education for Minors
- Right to Counsel
- Right to Habeas Corpus

The client does have a right to a certain standard of quality service but not minimum service.

The answer is **(D)**

Solution 36

A treatment plan is contingent on addressing the needs of the individual client. All of the screening process and information must be used to make determinations. Therefore, the treatment plan can only be developed after the screening process is complete.

The answer is **(A)**

Solution 37

The phases of the treatment process are usually engagement, stabilization, primary treatment and continuing care.

The answer is (B)

Solution 38

The engagement of the client in the development of the treatment process is essentially to have them feel they are actively participating and have some control over the process. However, the decisions of the treatment and diagnosis should come from professionals so that the right course of action can be established.

The answer is (A)

Solution 39

Treatment plans should indeed be reviewed on a regular basis. However, a new plan should only be developed if a client is readmitted (restarting the process) or a significant amount of time has occurred, often 1 year. The treatment plan should be consistent despite any problems that may occur along the way or any minor changes.

The answer is (C)

Solution 40

Acceptance, while an important part of the change in mentality that needs to occur for the progress of substance abuse, is not recognized as one of the six stages of change.

The answer is (B)

Solution 41

The treatment plan should always be flexible to continue to adapt to the individual based on how they react to any new information. It should not be rigid so that it can adjust when ineffective.

The answer is (A)

Solution 42

The ASAM criteria mainly states that the problems, strengths, goals, and progress must be identified. The amount or timeframe of any assessment of the process is not a part of the criteria.

The answer is (B)

Solution 43

An initial treatment plan is mainly based on the initial screening and information gathering. Something more in depth such as a diagnosis is not often included in the initial plan but certainly will be included in the individual plan

The answer is (D)

Solution 44

Goals and objectives should be determined as a part of the individual development plan. Both involve defining clear and achievable actions to complete during the process of recovery and must be measurable. Mainly the key difference is goals are a broader action that does not involve specifics. The objectives will include the more specific steps to achieve the goals.

The answer is (B)

Solution 45

Relapses are understood to be very common and unfortunately, a client can revert back to an earlier stage of progress. Most often this is a stage of contemplation where they need to again mentally prepare themselves to take action.

The answer is (B)

Solution 46

While there is typically a progression to the client's path through the stages, there may be movement throughout the cycle. The path one takes should not be seen as linear since they may jump all around throughout their journey

The answer is (C)

Solution 47

As the client progresses there are important steps they need to make in their mental state in order make the leap to taking action towards recovery. While recognizing substance abuse as a problem and seeing the adverse effect on a person's life is a necessary step, it is still a part of the contemplation stage. It is not until the person understands that the path of abuse is no longer outweighing the disadvantages substances are creating in their life.

The answer is (C)

Solution 48

When a client is in the action stage, this is when change to substance habits most often will occur and therefore is when withdrawal is most prevalent.

The answer is (C)

Solution 49

When collaborating with other agencies, it is imperative to be speaking the same language and evaluate under the same rules. Therefore a consistency should exist for assessment.

The answer is (A)

Solution 50

A primary agency shall act as the hub through which the standards for assessment are determined and communication flows. They should not designate any other agency as the main contact as they are responsible for this. While they will establish the common assessment criteria, the other agency will provide their input in their own area of expertise.

The answer is (A)

Solution 51

Case management has many advantages and purposes, but all must have the following four: Care that is consistent and continuous, accessibility, accountability, and efficiency

The answer is **(D)**

Solution 52

A case management system must consist of a Case manager and an assigned core agency.

The answer is **(A)**

Solution 53

While Rosenheck, Neale and Mohamed establish Low Intensity, there is no High Intensity case management approach.

The answer is **(B)**

Solution 54

Case management must adhere to the established principles to be successful. These principles are:

- Be the single point of contact
- Ensure the process is client driven and strength based
- Advocate for the client
- Involve the community
- Case management must adapt to be practical
- Anticipate problems and have a plan for resolution
- Be aware of cultural sensitivities

Case management should indeed be flexible when needed to adapt to the changing process or as new information becomes available. Therefore, case management should not be rigid.

The answer is **(B)**

Solution 55

While a client's needs are paramount for the success of the recovery process, you should not engage in advocating for anything illegal despite the wishes of the client.

The answer is **(C)**

Solution 56

The key elements as per Cross 1989 are

- Valuing diversity
- Making a cultural assessment
- Understanding cultural interaction dynamics
- Incorporating cultural knowledge
- Adapting practices to the diversity present in a setting

The answer is **(C)**

Solution 57

Case management needs to understand the health and safety of a client come first. However, this cannot go on to a point where the help is enabling the client to survive dependently. There is a point at which the process needs to move towards treatment and a self-sufficient life style.

The answer is **(B)**

Solution 58

Case managers while they should be aware of the ability to identify someone as a substance abuser, do not need this skill as an essential part of their role.

The answer is **(A)**

Solution 59

While it is most desirable to have the client actively engage and set up referred agencies, this may not always be the case. This is common if there is a prerequisite reason needed for admission such as a medical facility.

The answer is **(A)**

Solution 60

Typically, physical therapy and legal assistance is not provided by a substance abuse agency and is outside of their scope.

The answer is **(B)**

Solution 61

Short term goals, while may help to achieve the long-term goals, are not a necessary part of the service plan.

The answer is **(B)**

Solution 62

Referrals are often derailed by either the client's unwillingness or high expectations and poor coordination between agencies. All of the answers listed can be potential points of failure

The answer is **(D)**

Solution 63

A case manager often must act as both a facilitator of case management and an advocate for the client. The two roles are important but should have a distinct difference. A facilitator ensures the teams are organized and stay on track. Therefore, team meetings, coordination, and determining discussion topics fall under the facilitator role. The advocate role ensures the client is making progress and that their needs are met.

The answer is **(C)**

Solution 64

Developing personal relationships between agencies and understanding the process will certainly go a long way to successful case management. The personal relationships of the client however should not enter the equation as you do not want biased opinions to be present.

The answer is **(D)**

Solution 65

Evaluating if the process of case management is working is important to adjusting future services. Commonly the evaluation is done by determining the client's satisfaction, evaluating the outcome of the client's treatment, or by evaluating the outcomes of the system.

The answer is **(A)**

Solution 66

In almost all cases, information cannot be shared without a client's consent to another party. One major exception is the sharing of information for the Health Insurance Portability and Accountability Act (HIPAA) for uses of payment.

A co-worker may receive information on a need to know basis but only if they are a part of the treatment team.

The answer is **(A)**

Solution 67

Proper documentation is essential for many purposes including continuity of care, evaluation of processes, and legal defense. While it is important to foster relationships with third parties, documentation should only be shared as necessary and with the client's consent.

The answer is **(D)**

Solution 68

In some circumstances it may be common to keep records longer than the minimums for minors.

The answer is **(A)**

Solution 69

Section 2.65-e provides guideline on the content of the order when it is to be provided. There is no requirement regarding the public interest.

The answer is **(D)**

Solution 70

Documents must meet a certain standard, but these standards may be defined by many different entities. There is State authority, accreditation bodies which ensure a minimum level of service, third party payers which want to ensure they are paying for proper service, and provider agencies. Medical services while essential do not control the standard of documentation.

The answer is **(C)**

Solution 71

When gathering progress notes, a common method is the SO/AP or Subjective-Objective/Assessment-Plan. SO observations are facts about what happened. AP is an assessment of the facts during the session. In this case trying to diagnose the client as having co-occurring disorder would be an assessment and not just a statement of fact. Therefore, this is an AP progress note.

The answer is **(B)**

Solution 72

A discharge plan should contain the following:

- Referral source
- Problem statement
- Treatment goals, objectives, and outcome
- State of client upon completion of service
- Recommendations
- Final signatures

An exit interview is not an essential part.

The answer is **(D)**

Solution 73

In general, good writing for record keeping should be kept to facts about observations as much as possible. Inferring opinions or making judgements should be avoided.

Using jargon or slang should also be avoided, in this case the term shady is not very descriptive or even clear.

While the relationship with a significant other is important to note, it should be kept to facts and observations about their interactions.

It is also important to be positive if possible. Negative language can be detrimental to the process.

The answer is **(A)**

Solution 74

Errors should be noted in the document with a date and initial. They should not be removed as a record of the error is important to note.

The answer is **(D)**

Solution 75

Recovery management refers to the plan to avoid a relapse and reimplement the client into a healthy lifestyle within the community. Stabilizing the client's symptoms and drug use is a part of primary care that must occur so that treatment can proceed. It is not a part of recovery management.

The answer is **(A)**

Solution 76

Avoidance and mental toughness are necessary during recovery management. The client should re-establish their life and wellness and stay away from situations where those substances are present. While having peers to lean on is important, it is generally not a good idea to continue relationships for the client with those who continue to use.

The answer is **(B)**

Solution 77

The developmental model has stabilization as the second stage. Before any progress can be made, the client needs to return to a functioning state and therefore must first recover from withdrawal symptoms

The answer is **(C)**

Solution 78

Middle recovery's main goal is repairing one's lifestyle and social structure.

The answer is **(B)**

Solution 79

The path to relapse is often a gradual progression of deterioration in behavior and will. All of these signs should be noted and intervened with if identified. The first warning sign may likely come in a change of the daily structure.

The answer is **(A)**

Solution 80

While a client must be mentally strong to have control over their own mental state, it is inevitable that thoughts of having a drink or using a drug will enter into one's mind. The appropriate action is not to resist but learn how to manage these thoughts. It is likely these thoughts will never go away, and the client needs to be prepared on how to handle them when they do arrive

The answer is **(A)**

Solution 81

There have been shifts in philosophy in the defining of the recovery process. It originally was looked at as reaching abstinence and then continuing isolated treatments by professionals. Now the focus is on the long-term solution of self-growth and wellness.

The answer is **(D)**

Solution 82

The harm reduction model realizes that abstinence may not be an obtainable goal and the philosophy is to reduce the effects of substance abuse wherever possible.

The answer is **(D)**

Solution 83

While the traditional 12-step program offers many benefits, it is not for everyone. The type of abuse does not matter as there is AA or NA for whatever the substance used is. Of these, the client with social anxiety may not succeed in this type of program. They are required to speak publicly and share in front of people they have never met. If this may be seen as detrimental to progress, an alternative may be appropriate.

The answer is **(A)**

Solution 84

There is a wide range of triggers which can set someone off on a path to relapse. It can be negative events in one's life that leads to feelings of sadness or despair. A person may also be reminded of the feelings of drug use by the senses. It could be as mundane as a smell or a song that was played during drug use. Often overlooked is the positive events that could be a trigger. During times of celebration, people often let their guard down and may be prone to a relapse.

The answer is **(D)**

Solution 85

There are 12 principles as per the Substance Abuse and Mental Health Services Administration. Among them is the need for support from peers and allies. However, the direction of professional help is not a requirement. The focus is mainly on the physical and mental state of the self.

The answer is **(B)**

Solution 86

Most individuals do not seek out professional help. It is estimated that about 3 out of 4 people who are recovering from substance abuse did not.

The answer is **(B)**

Solution 87

The therapeutic alliance is a focus on the relationship between the client and the counselor. While the counselor should ensure a good relationship with any others involved in the process, the alliance is built through agreement and connection with the client.

The answer is **(B)**

Solution 88

While the counselor should use experience to guide the conversation or make observations, the client should know that their experience is unique and their path both through abuse and to recovery is unique. A counselor should not impose a different client's experience on another.

The answer is **(D)**

Solution 89

Motivational interviewing should employ five principles

- Show empathy
- Evaluate how a client's behavior is affecting their goals
- Avoid confrontation
- Adjust to client resistance
- Provide optimism

An argument should be avoided if possible.

The answer is **(B)**

Solution 90

For a client with co-occurring disorders, many of the techniques used normally can still be very effective. However, they may need to be adjusted to adapt to the specific needs of the client. Clients with co-occurring disorders will often have difficulty concentrating or retaining information. Therefore, repetition in an appropriate way is very important to ensure the intention is understood.

The answer is **(A)**

Solution 91

The client, and people in general, can often have a skewed view of the past or how it actually felt during those experiences. Helping him to remember exactly how it felt may be an effective way to stop a potential relapse. Often boredom can be a significant trigger. A healthier lifestyle should include something to fill this void as well.

The answer is **(D)**

Solution 92

While the counselor should indeed evaluate a group that best fits the needs of the client, the client needs to be consulted in the process so that a match is found.

The answer is **(A)**

Solution 93

Motivational interviewing is essentially about forming a partnership that allows the client to thrive. The element not listed here is evocation. The client needs to build from within to become a better person and the counselor should encourage this. Intervening is not a part of the process.

The answer is **(D)**

Solution 94

The client needs to understand the rules of the session. Most are basic logistics such as being on time or respectful. It should not be appropriate however for the client to arrive at a session under the influence. These sessions should be canceled and then evaluated.

The answer is **(C)**

Solution 95

The spiritual model notes that the cause of abuse is related to someone's own character and how they may use substances to fill the emptiness of their life.

The answer is **(B)**

Solution 96

Self-disclosure can be a tricky technique to navigate. It most certainly can help to build a strong relationship and establish trust. However, it may be detrimental if not handled properly. The focus should remain on the client and getting too detailed or talkative about your own life may not be the best idea.

The answer is **(B)**

Solution 97

Empathy can be one of the most impactful skills a counselor can develop. It often fosters a connection with the client that will lead to trust and success in the process. It is important however to distinguish empathy from sympathy. Empathy is understanding a person's feelings and experiences. Sympathy expresses sorrow for another person.

The answer is **(A)**

Solution 98

All of these listed are indeed evidence-based therapy examples. SAMSHA provides a registry of these practices.

The answer is **(D)**

Solution 99

Short term treatment options will typically last less than six months. Of the options, residential communities are designed to surround the client with a social structure that will create a new lifestyle. This can often take a significant amount of time.

The answer is **(C)**

Solution 100

The main goal of withdrawal management is to ensure the eradication of the toxins from the client in a safe manner. There is a significant risk for the health of the client and possible others during the process. This should be the only goal at the time and any evaluation of the client should wait.

The answer is **(B)**

Solution 101

Of the options listed, outpatient treatment may be used for people who have difficulty leaving the home. It is often costlier so those who are unemployed may not be able to take advantage. A residential treatment often is for someone who has had a deteriorated social structure and would otherwise be alone.

The answer is **(A)**

Solution 102

Methadone, also known as Methadose, has been found to help treat opioid addiction in some cases. Disulfiram and Acamprosate are used for alcohol addiction.

The answer is **(A)**

Solution 103

A psychoeducational group's main purpose is to provide the client with the information they need to progress through treatment.

The answer is **(A)**

Solution 104

At this time the FDA has not approved the use of any medications for medication-assisted treatment for methamphetamines.

The answer is **(C)**

Solution 105

A crisis and the need to intervene is dependent on the client's mental state. Having a stressful event occur does not necessarily create a crisis but the reaction by the client is most important. The altering of the mental state will cause the client to potential spiral into a problematic state.

The answer is **(B)**

Solution 106

While relapse prevention is important to the future well-being of the client, crisis intervention needs to focus on the present problem at hand to deescalate the situation to a normal state. It is not a necessary step in crisis intervention.

The answer is **(D)**

Solution 107

A crisis intervention must focus on the present or at most the immediate past. Regular counseling will dive into the history of the client, but here the goal is to have the situation subside. Using verbal de-escalation and establishing a rapport are important steps to achieving a resolution.

It is also recommended to meet in person if at all possible. The non-verbal communication and presence carry weight in the conversation.

The answer is **(A)**

Solution 108

The HALT acronym identifies emotional dangers that should be recognized as potential triggers. The "T" stands for Tired, not temptation.

The answer is **(D)**

Solution 109

Relapse prevention in general has a focus on the changing of one's lifestyle to healthy and positive changes which set a strong foundation to ward off triggers and temptation.

The answer is **(B)**

Solution 110

Relapse prevention therapy concentrates on coping and prevention skills necessary to be prepared throughout the process of a relapse. It does not want the process to end abruptly. A client should both learn from a relapse and stay engaged in treatment.

The answer is **(D)**

Solution 111

Relapse prevention therapy focuses on cognitive and behavioral techniques. Cognitive may include reflecting on relapses and learning from experiences. Behavioral are implementing changes to one's lifestyle that may have a positive impact such as meditation or prayer.

The answer is **(B)**

Solution 112

The CENAPS Model views addiction as a disease and strives for the client to be completely abstinent along with positive changes in one's lifestyle. There are five main components:

- Assessment
- Warning Sign Identification
- Warning Sign Management
- Recovery Planning
- Relapse Early Intervention Training

The answer is **(D)**

Solution 113

CENAPS and the Marlatt and Gordon model have many similarities. The key difference is that the CENAPS model uses abstinence-based treatment.

The answer is **(A)**

Solution 114

Triggers can involve many different events, actions or emotions. They also will vary from person to person, so it is important to treat each client individually to determine what triggers may be most at risk. The most common however, are unpleasant emotions, interpersonal conflict, or social pressure.

The answer is **(C)**

Solution 115

Evidence based practices provide scientific evidence of why certain treatments may work. This can guide or provide persuasion to use certain treatment plans. The goal is not to eradicate other means of treatment but rather to help the process as a whole.

The answer is **(A)**

Solution 116

Implementation of a new practice is not a simple process and requires an integration of staff and philosophies. The clients however do not provide an opinion on the implementation but would rather provide input into if the program once implemented.

The answer is **(B)**

Solution 117

Fidelity is the loss of the intention of the evidence-based practice. It can be affected by failure to follow through on the procedures or being gradually tweaked over time. It can also be affected by different settings or situations.

The answer is **(D)**

Solution 118

Cognitive behavioral therapy focuses on the person's internal reactions to their outside world. The feelings and emotions that trigger abuse come from the interpretation of circumstances and not the events themselves.

The answer is **(B)**

Solution 119

Motivational enhancement proposes to quicken the process through intense initial assessment. This includes battery and individual sessions in a rapid pace.

The answer is **(A)**

Solution 120

Trauma-informed approaches include providing information about potential traumas and how to handle them. Trauma-specific approaches deal with treating the effects from a specific event that caused the trauma. Therefore, someone enrolling in a program to address a specific issue falls under trauma-specific

The answer is **(C)**

Solution 121

The family disease model looks at substance abuse as a disease that may have an impact on the individuals of the family. This may often lead to codependence.

The answer is **(A)**

Solution 122

When adjusting models for cultural reasons, there are two types of changes. Cultural accommodation is modifying how the model is delivered for better understanding or accommodation. Cultural adaptation changes the actual structure of the model for cultural reasons.

The answer is **(B)**

Solution 123

It is important to understand the difficulty others who are affected by the substance abuser have in the process. It is often hard to let a loved one struggle or suffer but the long-term consequences must be considered. It is not a good idea to clean up any "messes" created from the substance abuse and that includes any damage to existing relationships

The answer is **(A)**

Solution 124

The traditional means of measuring progress was based on the recognition of the completion of goals. There was no tracking of data in the progress of the client. Therefore, it is classified as a qualitative assessment.

The answer is **(A)**

Solution 125

Regardless of whether or not an individual has HIV/AIDS, there is a greater risk of mental health issues as compared to the general population.

The answer is **(B)**

Solution 126

Because of the challenges and barriers a disability may cause, a person with a physical disability is less likely to seek treatment than others.

The answer is **(A)**

Solution 127

The precedence from highest to lowest is as follows:

- Law
- Precedent by case law
- Common Sense
- Administrative rule
- Contracts

Nothing supersedes Federal or State law

The answer is **(D)**

Solution 128

The principles of trauma-informed care can be summarized as:

- Understanding trauma and its effects
- Safety
- Help the client to regain control
- Sharing of power
- Cultural sensitivities
- Integrating care
- Establishing or repairing relationships
- Ensuring the possibility of recovery

Within these, a single source of decision making does not fit. There should be collaboration and team input

The answer is **(B)**

Solution 129

HIPPAA protects the clients right to privacy and information regarding themselves. It does not apply to other documents outside of their own record.

The answer is **(C)**

Solution 130

As per SAMSHA's National Survey on Drug Use, men are more likely to be given an opportunity to use drugs for the first time, but once that opportunity occurs, they are equally likely to try the drug. It is also proven that the effects of drugs for women are different than they are for men, but more males suffer from SUD than women. Among youths however, the numbers for women vs. men is about equal.

The answer is **(A)**

Solution 131

While much of a code of ethics can be agreed upon by separate entities, there is no universally accepted code of ethics.

The answer is **(A)**

Solution 132

There are three elements of morality. They are the counselor as a person, a moral sense, and values.

The counselor as a person appeals to the counselors understanding of right and wrong through their own experiences and life events.

Moral sense is an innate sense of right and wrong that develops throughout one's life.

Values refer to what is important in a person's life.

In this question, the feeling of something not being right relates to an inner moral sense.

The answer is **(B)**

Solution 133

Corey et al. defines the six guidelines of daily ethical conduct as:

- Provide informed consent
- Operate in a competent manner
- Ensure confidentiality
- Maintain appropriate relationship boundaries
- Utilize adequate consultation
- Honor personal and cultural values

The answer is **(D)**

Solution 134

To provide informed consent, a client must be of stable mind to think rationally, must understand the issue at hand, and must not be held against their will. There is no consultation requirement.

The answer is **(C)**

Solution 135

The Code of Federal regulations which covers confidentiality includes the three answers listed as potential ways to release a client's information.

The answer is **(D)**

Solution 136

42 CFR has many provisions. They do not apply differently if an employee is no longer with or involved in a company

The answer is **(A)**

Solution 137

A consent form must include all pertinent information however, the date of any consultation is not required. The consent form shall include the date of signature, but this is not necessarily the same activity.

The answer is **(D)**

Solution 138

It is important to maintain boundaries and have a clearly defined role in the client's life. In general, avoiding any relationship outside of the professional environment is encouraged. Even contact which may be perceived as harmless can be dangerous at times.

It is also important to remember to not let biases creep into counseling. The client's individuality must be considered, and it is inappropriate to push something that has worked for the counselor.

The answer is **(C)**

Solution 139

The five stages of cultural competence are:

- Destructiveness
- Incapacity
- Blindness
- Pre-competence
- Competence

The answer is **(D)**

Solution 140

An adult who needs to have discussions about substance abuse should be educated and prepared to have a productive talk. Developing a plan of action and mentally preparing one's self to be calm and constructive. While the child should indeed take responsibility for actions, passing blame on the child is not the best approach. They should not feel as though they are being attacked and it is counterintuitive to getting them to accept a path to recovery.

The answer is **(B)**

Solution 141

When evaluating the impact of cultural considerations on a specific client's issues, it is important to not use stereotypes by any means. Generalizations however can be an acceptable way to begin the investigation into facts and then a determination can be made. A stereotype by definition determines facts up front without investigating evidence. Generalizations are common trends which can be used as a basis.

The answer is **(C)**

Solution 142

The final stage of cultural competence is competence and proficiency. At this point one can recognize that culturally responsive practices should be implemented. These stages are more of a mental transformation and is not related to the actual implementation.

The answer is **(B)**

Solution 143

The methods listed are all options for furthering the practice of cultural sensitivity.

The answer is **(D)**

Solution 144

The time that adolescents are most vulnerable is often when a major life transition occurs. The person is exposed to new peers and experiences that may be difficult to handle. There is no one transition that can be identified as the clear most difficult and precautions need to be taken along the entire process.

The answer is **(D)**

Solution 145

It is important to consider the specific audience when prevention programs are being considered.

Universal – A attempt to reduce risks of alcohol or substance abuse across a general population

Selective – An attempt to reduce risk of alcohol and substance abuse for a specific family or group.

Indicated – An attempt to reduce risk in those already using alcohol or substances

The answer is **(C)**

Solution 146

The DEA classifies drugs into five different categories called schedules. The categories range from the most addictive (category I) to the least potential for addiction (category V). Of the options, mescaline, also known as peyote, is considered category I.

The answer is **(C)**

Solution 147

Of the options listed, inhalants have not been identified as having a connection with successful behavioral treatment.

The answer is **(A)**

Solution 148

While it is certainly not an acceptable choice, using mescaline in combination with alcohol does not have any identified additional effects.

The answer is **(A)**

Solution 149

While the initial concern may be that it is indeed better for individuals to make the choice to come to treatment, it is not often that a person with SUD will freely admit to this. Legally mandated treatment takes some choices away from the individual and creates a higher chance for attendance and longevity of treatment.

The answer is **(C)**

Solution 150

Marijuana does have some long-term effects. One of the more severe concerns can be chronic bronchitis.

The answer is **(B)**

Solution 151

The stages which occur in order are:

- Recognition of potential risk
- Initial screening
- Comprehensive assessment
- Interventions
- Process evaluation and outcome determination

There is no secondary screening

The answer is **(C)**

Solution 152

It is often difficult for family or peers to definitively decide that someone they know has a clear problem. Because of this, it is very often the case that an unfortunate event which clearly indicates there is a problem will be the impetus for the recognition of risk. Sometimes this can develop slowly over time, but it is often needed for the person addicted to have an undisputable indicator that there is an issue

The answer is **(A)**

Solution 153

Any changes to the normal tendencies or established trends in someone's life should be flagged as a potential concern for someone at risk. This may be noticeable changes in schedule or uncommon behavior at school or work. Consistent medical issues can also be a clear sign given the effects of substances.

The answer is **(D)**

Solution 154

To properly perform a drug recognition technique, one should note any clear physical or behavioral signs of substance abuse. Then determine, based on knowledge, the potential type of substance being used. However, before moving on, you must try to rule out any other physical or medical issue that may be causing the identified signs. There may be other factors at work that will cause similar signs as substance abuse.

The answer is **(A)**

Solution 155

When gathering information, the three sources are existing information, interviews, and any testing. While observing someone in the field or their natural environment would be beneficial, it is not a practical means of gathering information.

The answer is **(C)**

Solution 156

Data gathering should be reserved to factual evidence of one's history that can be documented. This would relate to any medical (family or individual), criminal, or employment history. The current mental state should be determined from observed and recent interactions with the client.

The answer is **(A)**

Solution 157

The Comprehensive Drinker Profile is a structured interview for the purpose of gathering information regarding drinking history.

The answer is **(D)**

Solution 158

Counseling is used to explore a problem and identify potential solutions through investigations and expression of thoughts and feelings. At this point however, a problem has been identified and established.

The answer is **(A)**

Solution 159

It is important to provide effective and appropriate feedback when counseling. Feedback should not be overly general. It should address some specific aspect of the conversation that is actionable or notable.

The answer is **(B)**

Solution 160

Of the options listed, marijuana is not a central nervous system stimulant.

The answer is **(C)**

Solution 161

When using reflective listening, it is important to avoid imposing your own thoughts on the client. While all of the phrases are very similar, the first indicates that the counselor already has determined how the client feels and is not investigating it further.

The answer is **(A)**

Solution 162

The Johari Window is a model which classifies information based on the extent the information is known by an individual or by others. Open is more general information known by all and by one's self. In general, this is where the level of self-disclosure should remain. If relevant, a counselor may choose to volunteer information that many do not know. But this should be evaluated as to the usefulness of the disclosure.

The answer is **(A)**

Solution 163

Interpreting is mainly used to provide the client with a different point of view on an issue to help understanding or motivation.

The answer is **(B)**

Solution 164

Confrontation should be used carefully but can be very effective. It should be employed if the client is not coming to terms with something that can be clearly identified or observed otherwise. All of the examples provided are consistent with this and therefore are all appropriate.

The answer is **(D)**

Solution 165

There are five types associated with blocking behavior which can be disruptive to group settings. They are summarized as:

- Type 1 – Client doesn't feel they relate to others in the group
- Type 2 – Client does not move from thoughts to expressing feeling
- Type 3 – Client willingly irritates others
- Type 4 – Client causes confusion
- Type 5 – Client arrives under the influence of a substance

The answer is **(A)**

Solution 166

An alcoholic family is a detrimental dynamic to all of its members. The family actions are centered around the alcoholism and the resulting consequences. The family does not however shy away from protecting the alcoholic and will often do that which enables further destruction.

The answer is **(C)**

Solution 167

A treatment plan needs to be flexible and adapt to the progress made by a client. To ensure this flexibility, regular review is recommended. Every day would be extreme but once per week is often appropriate enough.

The answer is **(B)**

Solution 168

There are four types of traumas which can elicit a crisis. They are:

Situational – A traumatic event occurring such as a death in the family
Developmental – Events related to growing up
Intrapsychic – Thoughts and emotions impacting one's actions
Existential – A sense of one's place in the world. Not knowing one's purpose

Peer pressure and how to handle it are a part of growing up and is in the developmental category.

The answer is **(B)**

Solution 169

While it may be tempting to assure the client that everything will be ok, making light of the reality of the situation will most often result in a long-term detrimental effect. If it does not work out well, the trust with the client may be broken. Being honest, even when it is not pleasant, is important.

The answer is **(B)**

Solution 170

Suicide is a very delicate situation and there needs to be a plan ready to implement if needed. The focus should be on understanding the client and what has caused the thoughts. Getting them to postpone so you can talk is a good goal. You should not shift focus from the issue or tell them what great things are in life. This creates a sense of misunderstanding and will potentially drive them further away.

The answer is **(A)**

Solution 171

The core intention for a referral is to seek help that can only be found outside of an agency that addresses an identified client issue.

The answer is **(A)**

Solution 172

The stages progress from experimental to abuse and then to dependency. The defining characteristic of the final stage is the person's distress upon not using the substance. This physiological change shows that there has been significant damage to the individual's physical and mental state.

The answer is **(B)**

Solution 173

It is important to have an understanding of the different ways cultures may view the world. Some Asian-Americans, for example, may see the community or group around them as more important than the individual and may be willing to sacrifice aspects of themselves which may be beyond other viewpoints. This is known as Community oriented worldview.

The answer is **(C)**

Solution 174

When being culturally sensitive, be careful to not automatically assume an individual follows all generalizations of a culture. Especially for the first meeting of a client, do not assume they greet or act in a certain way.

The answer is **(C)**

Solution 175

There are three different clusters as per DSM-5

Cluster A -Eccentric behavior such as paranoid or schizoid

Cluster B – Dramatic or emotional behavior

Cluster C – Fearful behavior

Paranoia falls under cluster A.

The answer is **(A)**

Solution 176

Federal laws if applicable will supersede state law unless the state law is stricter. Federal laws however will only apply if the program is federally assisted.

The answer is **(C)**

Solution 177

For a parent or guardian to be contacted without the consent of the minor, all of the items listed need to be present.

The answer is **(D)**

Solution 178

It is not appropriate to use a general timeframe for the consent of information. The individual specifics of the case should be considered and a decision reached.

The answer is **(D)**

Solution 179

The "Duty to Warn" is the obligation of a counselor to take action and break confidentiality if the client indicates the potential for an act of violence against a specified individual. It does not apply to nonspecific victims. Also, it only applies to the client themselves being involved.

The answer is **(B)**

Solution 180

According to general statistics only 1 suicide attempt is successful per every 25 attempts.

The answer is **(D)**

Solution 181

At the point the BAC reaches about 0.2 (or about 7 standard drinks) it is difficult to function if the body has not developed a tolerance for alcohol equal to that of alcoholics. A normal person could see serious medical issues at this level. It can be used then as an indicator of someone suffering from substance abuse.

The answer is **(B)**

Solution 182

REM sleep is the period of recovery for the body. Heavy drinking greatly effects the body's ability to reach this state and therefore causes the user to have a poor quality of sleep.

The answer is **(A)**

Solution 183

The level of care quadrants are classified into four categories. Each is some combination of the severity of the mental health disorder and the substance abuse. For more severe mental health and less severe substance abuse, the client would be in category II.

The answer is **(B)**

Solution 184

HIV is transmitted through bodily fluids which include blood, semen, vaginal secretions, and breast milk. Sneezing or cough does not transmit the disease.

The answer is **(A)**

Solution 185

If a client has been free of meeting the criteria for three months but not more than 12, then they are said to be in early remission.

The answer is **(C)**

Solution 186

Increased pupil size is commonly associated with withdrawal from opiate drugs.

The answer is **(C)**

Solution 187

An important factor in recovery is immediately engaging the client in treatment after detoxification. They are in a difficult and vulnerable state after the pain of detoxification and need to be set on the correct path immediately.

The answer is **(A)**

Solution 188

AA subscribes to the mindset of understanding the things that cannot be controlled. Therefore, they will teach to admit powerlessness and understand the influence substances have over a person.

The answer is **(A)**

Solution 189

While we do not want to think of money as an issue, it does become a factor sometimes in treatment. Individual treatment is more expensive than other forms.

The answer is **(B)**

Solution 190

Peer participation groups provide activities and roles in the community that can give the abuser some responsibility and healthy distraction from the draws of substances.

The answer is **(D)**

Solution 191

The goal in handling cocaine withdrawal is to stave off cravings long enough for the symptoms to subside. All of the drugs listed can be used to counteract the effects.

The answer is **(D)**

Solution 192

Aversive conditioning is using negative reinforcement to associate it with unwanted behavior or thoughts. This may be used to associate the thoughts or images of substances with some negative reaction. This method to some has been thought to be successful but further research is required.

The answer is **(A)**

Solution 193

Intake is the administrative and initial procedures of taking a client into care. Once the screening is complete, this begins the actual process of treatment.

The answer is **(B)**

Solution 194

Confidentiality is something that occurs upfront and should occur during the intake phase.

The answer is **(A)**

Solution 195

Interpreting as a counseling skill helps in clarification of the relationship between the client and the counselor. It is not used to break down any barriers that the client may have shown

The answer is **(B)**

Solution 196

This is an example of a client saying one thing but then contradicting it with a later statement.

The answer is **(C)**

Solution 197

When dealing with confrontation the client can have a number of responses including resistance or anger. When the client acts appropriately in a manner that will be constructive to progress, it is important to reinforce the behavior by commending the good reaction.

The answer is **(C)**

Solution 198

Showing expertise provides a skill that others in the group do not have and therefore must respect. This gives the leader a sense of authority and will be able to make decisions that the group will follow.

The answer is **(A)**

Solution 199

A negative test result does not automatically mean someone is in the clear. There is a time period between the time the disease in passed and the presence of the antibody which will trigger the positive result. It can take months or even in rare cases a year to show up.

The answer is **(D)**

Solution 200

A client who does not accept being at fault or wrong can be detrimental to their progress and are characterized as self-righteous.

The answer is **(B)**

Solution 201

Basic needs must be addressed first before treatment can begin. These include any medical problems, mental health, or the client's ability to find food or shelter.

The answer is **(D)**

Solution 202

Physiological refers to the natural function of the body. Having a fear of the pain from withdrawal appeals to this need.

The answer is **(A)**

Solution 203

The termination of counseling process should only begin if the counselor feels the client has achieved their goals and clearly exhibits appropriate character traits that indicate independence and an ability to live a healthy lifestyle. Philosophical differences or disagreements are not a reason to terminate.

The answer is **(B)**

Solution 204

Boundaries and rules are important to establish proper discipline in sessions where needed. Setting times and frequencies are appropriate however you should not limit what the client wishes to explore.

The answer is **(C)**

Solution 205

In general, Asian Americans have the lowest rate of use at around 28%

The answer is **(D)**

Solution 206

Studies show in general the LGB population is more likely to use alcohol and drugs by percentage.

The answer is **(A)**

Solution 207

People from rural populations are more isolated than those in urban. This may often lead to more independence and individuality. They may be more private and therefore emotions may be held in more often.

The answer is **(D)**

Solution 208

There is a very strong connection between the homeless population and disorders. About two-thirds of those have the connection.

The answer is **(C)**

Solution 209

It is important to be aware of client resistance which may not always come in the form of confrontation. It can be subtler including interrupting and ignoring.

The answer is **(D)**

Solution 210

In this situation, the counselor feels the appropriate topic is not being discussed and is shifting to a new topic.

The answer is **(C)**

Solution 211

Showing agreement is a good way to show the client you are listening, and it validates their opinion. It can be effective to then make a valid point after the agreement. This is called agreement with a twist

The answer is **(D)**

Solution 212

In this case the client is shifting the blame for his own actions to others.

The answer is **(A)**

Solution 213

Open-ended questions lead the client to think and explore their own emotions and feelings. They are not yes are no answer questions. Asking if someone is angry, while discussing emotions, does not lead to exploration and can be answered by a yes or no.

The answer is **(A)**

Solution 214

When a client has a realization than can then in turn motivate them to moving forward, it is classified as self-motivational.

The answer is **(C)**

Solution 215

Process recognition is not one of the four.

The answer is **(C)**

Solution 216

Cocaine use can is often characterized as binges until all of the available supply is depleted. This usually happens over a period of one to two days.

The answer is **(B)**

Solution 217

It is important to differentiate between the types of alcohol use so that you may identify inappropriate patterns. Alcohol misuse is defined as an inappropriate and not deliberate amount of consumption causing an altered state.

The answer is **(B)**

Solution 218

Reliability refers to the confidence you can have that an assessment tool does not have erroneous results.

The answer is **(A)**

Solution 219

An adolescent may revoke consent at any time and does not need agreement or permission from anyone.

The answer is **(D)**

Solution 220

During this transition, a client will begin to have their focus shift to the change in their lives instead of the current problem at hand. He may become more optimistic and ask different questions. They often will appear more peaceful and resolved. Being excitable or anxious is not associated with this change.

The answer is **(B)**

Solution 221

The preparation stage is all about getting ready to move forward with the process of treatment. Getting the client to believe they have a problem by means such as raising doubts is more often in the earlier stages of change.

The answer is **(A)**

Solution 222

Validity is a measure of the tests ability to produce meaningful results for its intention. When looking at assessment tests, there are four kinds of validity to be aware of:

Content – Looking at the results based on logical reasoning

Concurrent – Using a separate measure to compare the test results for an intended trait

Predictive – Assessment of future behavior

Construct – Whether the test results are consistent with the theory behind the test

The answer is **(B)**

Solution 223

Federal regulations indicate that only in the three scenarios listed in the question that consent may be given without the adolescent.

The answer is **(D)**

Solution 224

A client who is constantly talking or tries to always make the conversation about them is called a monopolizing client.

The answer is **(A)**

Solution 225

When dealing with intervention preparation, the family and friends must be on the same page as to the approach and intention of the event. Other issues the participants may have with the user should not take the focus away from the problem of substance abuse. It is most likely that the user will not seek help on their own and an intervention is necessary for action to be taken. Confrontation is also a delicate circumstance and should be anticipated. Those who do not feel comfortable dealing with it in a calm and constructive manner should refrain from doing so.

The answer is **(D)**

Solution 226

In the dependency stage, the user is taking somewhat severe actions to obtain the substance, but it is not yet at the level of any means necessary or criminal acts.

The answer is **(B)**

Solution 227

Quaaludes are no longer in legal use.

The answer is **(A)**

Solution 228

Of those listed, Cocaine is not a narcotic.

The answer is **(D)**

Solution 229

Narcotics can be both produced synthetically or occur naturally

Due to the sharing of needles for certain narcotics such as heroin, they are linked to AIDS

Some narcotics are legal for the medical uses of pain relief and cough suppression

The answer is **(A)**

Solution 230

Pain relief can be an effect of drug use, but it is not classified as a rewarding feeling that causes dopamine release and leads to addiction.

The answer is **(C)**

Solution 231

Learning that a certain action will create acceptance amongst one's peers relates to social learning. It is a new found understanding of the dynamics of a group and how substances are perceived.

The answer is **(A)**

Solution 232

There is no type of individualized treatment that is found to be consistently more effective than others.

The answer is **(B)**

Solution 233

Peer teaching programs are designed to have peers teach each other about substance abuse.

The answer is **(B)**

Solution 234

Women in general will typically have lower self esteem than men.

The answer is **(C)**

Solution 235

Maintaining a physical boundary can have an impact on the development of trust. It creates a separation that may subconsciously be detrimental to the formation of a bond.

The answer is **(A)**

Solution 236

The verbal assessment is an opportunity to gather as much information about the history of the client and their patterns of substance use.

The answer is **(D)**

Solution 237

While observing the physical appearance is an evaluation of physical traits, it is more an indication of the client's mental state. Therefore, this is classified as psychological attending

The answer is **(B)**

Solution 238

The counselor is making specific physical choices to ensure the comfort of the client. This is classified as physical attending.

The answer is **(A)**

Solution 239

As potentially violent or harmful situations arise, it is helpful to continue to interpret the client's feelings. They must feel as though their point is heard and understood. Often, a client feeling misunderstood is the source of the anger.

The answer is **(A)**

Solution 240

The client should not feel like they are running the sessions.

The answer is **(B)**

Solution 241

Using repetitive and predictable language is a common mistake and is called stereotypical language.

The answer is **(B)**

Solution 242

All these techniques are a way to show the client you are listening and can condense and clarify thoughts.

The answer is **(D)**

Solution 243

Direction is not essential when using probing.

The answer is **(B)**

Solution 244

The counselor should not rely on the client for ensuring the referral is working out. It is more effective to speak with the organization directly.

The answer is **(A)**

Solution 245

Regression is when a client reverts back to a more immature state. Staying in bed is avoiding a situation as a child would want to. The client is regressing back to a childlike state.

The answer is **(A)**

Solution 246

A number of definitions exist from different entities but there is no one specific definition.

The answer is **(D)**

Solution 247

For a substance to be addictive it must release dopamine in the brain. Caffeine does not do this and therefore is not an addictive substance.

The answer is **(A)**

Solution 248

There are so many benefits to quitting, but it takes a significant amount of time for the user to revert back to non-smoker levels of health. The risk of stroke is one such health effect that takes 5-15 years.

The answer is **(D)**

Solution 249

Reducing the drinking age as a preventative measure is directed at a general population and not a specific group. This can be considered Universal.

The answer is **(A)**

Solution 250

Motivational interviewing encompasses a wide range of techniques with the goal of encouraging and increasing client motivation to change. Drug information can help by means of education but is not specifically geared towards client motivation.

The answer is **(D)**

Solution 251

When discussing how the process will work, the client must understand the expectations for change. It does not often occur instantly and can be viewed a long process with hurdles and setbacks along the way.

The answer is **(B)**

Solution 252

The action stage is, as the name suggests, where steps are taken mentally, physically and socially towards actual lifestyle change. Announcing the plans for change, while can be motivating, is not a tangible action of change and does not fall in this stage.

The answer is **(A)**

Solution 253

When a client does not fully realize the detrimental effects of substance abuse on their life, it is extremely difficult to work towards recovery. This is a very common situation as it is difficult to see the entire picture of one's life when they are experiencing addiction.

The answer is **(A)**

Solution 254

When a client has a realization of the physical effects substance abuse can have on a person, this is an affective expression of change.

The answer is **(B)**

Solution 255

Counter-motivational statements are the antithesis of self-motivational statements. A client will begin to use self-motivational statements as they begin to accept and realize the affects of substance abuse. Counter-motivational statements are not productive and are a sign of a lack of progress. Continuing to recognize positive influences from substances is a clear sign of this.

The answer is **(A)**

Solution 256

The statement is trying to get the client to realize the problems substances can cause.

The answer is **(A)**

Solution 257

A client who is resisting the change needed can be classified as rebellious.

The answer is **(B)**

Solution 258

The ability of a client to be able to handle situations where they may be influenced to use is called coping.

The answer is **(A)**

Solution 259

Despite the usefulness of assessment tools, they are not to be used as the sole means of assessment.

The answer is **(A)**

Solution 260

For this client there is some significant concerns of harm or violence. They have not expressed intent or threats which is the identifier of the serious level of risk. This situation can be classified as moderate.

The answer is **(C)**

Solution 261

The M.I.N.I. interview provides a point system based on the client's answers to yes or no questions. The most severe being a client having a plan of action for suicide.

The answer is **(D)**

Solution 262

To determine if a client has a co-occurring disorder, it is necessary to isolate the potential disorder away from the substance abuse. 30 days of abstinence is a significant amount of time to determine if the co-occurring disorder may occur without substances.

The answer is **(A)**

Solution 263

Of the medications listed, Methadone is not formally approved.

The answer is **(A)**

Solution 264

The stability of a client's situation must be assessed when determining if they may take home medication for treatment assistance. All of the requirements listed should be met.

The answer is **(D)**

Solution 265

There are physical differences in women that cause differences in substance abuse. They will develop health problems due to substance abuse over shorter periods of time.

The answer is **(C)**

Solution 266

The options listed all are reasons that medication may need to be stopped. The effects of these drugs must be closely monitored so as not to have a detrimental effect.

The answer is **(D)**

Solution 267

Intensive outpatient treatment has similar goals and methods, but the frequency of interaction is increased to accelerate and provide consistency in the process.

The answer is **(B)**

Solution 268

People in jail who have substance abuse issues have to deal with many factors due to their situation. However, attendance is often mandatory and not as frequently an issue

The answer is **(B)**

Solution 269

The tasks to ensure a culturally competent environment must be evaluated at all levels. The organizational tasks are the broadest reaching and indicate the organizations overall mission and vision.

The answer is **(A)**

Solution 270

Some cultures will inherently feel guilty over alcohol consumption which would yield incorrect results for this test as it relates to substance abuse. The traditional Arab Muslim community falls under this classification.

The answer is **(C)**

Solution 271

Drug cultures, just like societal cultures, can have their own rules, normal practices, languages, roles, and dress among many other characteristics.

The answer is **(D)**

Solution 272

Of those listed, CNS depressants are used to treat anxiety.

The answer is **(B)**

Solution 273

Opioids are a common cause of death among substance abuse cases, more so than illegal drugs.

The answer is **(B)**

Solution 274

The therapeutic alliance is important and has an effect on all types on counseling styles not just psychodynamic.

The answer is **(C)**

Solution 275

A single trauma is characterized as effects from a single, isolated occurrence.

The answer is **(A)**

Solution 276

Termination should only be brought up towards the end of the process in the final stage. Prematurely bringing this up can have a negative effect on group mentality.

The answer is **(C)**

Solution 277

Having others relate to a situation can encourage participation and unity. It is called commonality.

The answer is **(D)**

Solution 278

A silent client may be a result of a number of issues whether it be internal or external. All of those listed is a potential cause.

The answer is **(D)**

Solution 279

Of those listed, teenage women are less likely to be at risk for suicide.

The answer is **(B)**

Solution 280

Delayed reactions to traumatic events will be more deep seeded issues which will reveal themselves at certain times. Mood swings which result from deeper pain that has not been addressed may take time to develop.

The answer is **(B)**

Solution 281

In the traditional 12-step program, it is first necessary for the participant to admit that they are powerless to the addiction.

The answer is **(C)**

Solution 282

The current practices are more centered around the individuality of the client. Using general labels such as asthmatic or psychotic is not recommended anymore.

The answer is **(A)**

Solution 283

Ambulatory treatment is administered in a setting in which the client does not reside. IOP is typically administered in an office setting.

The answer is **(A)**

Solution 284

Psychoeducational focuses on providing knowledge about substances and the effects of abuse.

The answer is **(B)**

Solution 285

Role playing can be classified as kinesthetic.

The answer is **(C)**

Solution 286

Pregnant women who are younger than 18, due to their lack of maturity and knowledge have a higher rate than any other age group.

The answer is **(A)**

Solution 287

At this point in the process, you are observing the client for signs of substance abuse. There is no need for treatment and thus no need for consent.

The answer is **(C)**

Solution 288

The MET is a rapid and intense process that tries to change a person's mindset internally. The client is not guided slowly through a step by step process.

The answer is **(B)**

Solution 289

All of the listed options are appropriate to be utilized after discharge from treatment and help to maintain sobriety.

The answer is **(D)**

Solution 290

For a decision to be an ethical dilemma, it must include the impact on other people. Therefore, it cannot be both internal and external.

The answer is **(A)**

Solution 291

The effect of alcohol on each person is very different. It depends on many factors which includes all those listed.

The answer is **(D)**

Solution 292

Rohypnol is an extreme sedative that renders the user unable to move or remember during a certain period of time. It is not known for causing hallucinations.

The answer is **(D)**

Solution 293

A job is giving the client a way to contribute to society and have a sense of purpose.

The answer is **(B)**

Solution 294

Personal recovery capital is anything necessary for the well being of the client. Problem solving skills do not fall under this category.

The answer is **(B)**

Solution 295

While screening may take a number of steps in the appropriate direction for the client, the overall goal is to determine the need for additional assessment since the evidence suggests that there is a likely hood of substance abuse.

The answer is **(B)**

Solution 296

Breath, saliva and sweat are more short-term options. Hair can detect drug use over a much longer period of time.

The answer is **(B)**

Solution 297

A drug test is not a practical means of determining the need for medical attention. The counselor should identify other physical signs and act as quickly as possible.

The answer is **(C)**

Solution 298

A person with personality disorder will have difficulty in relationships and how they see themselves.

The answer is **(C)**

Solution 299

Specific goals give the client identifiable ideas to work towards and should be included.

The answer is **(D)**

Solution 300

A tangible and identifiable change can be classified as a client outcome

The answer is **(B)**

Solution 301

Of the most common substances in abuse, alcohol tends to be the most likely to cause harm on others, often times more so than the user.

The answer is **(A)**

Solution 302

Different methods for using a substance will travel through the body and to the brain at different rates. The least efficient is ingestion which has to be digested and can take between 20 – 90 minutes for the effect to be realized. Snorting is much shorter but still has to be absorbed into the nasal passages and can take 3 – 5 minutes. Injection into the blood stream is very fast and the substance travels to the brain in 15 – 30 seconds. The fastest however is smoking which will be absorbed and moved within 7 – 10 seconds.

The answer is **(C)**

Solution 303

The following are quick descriptions of the individual sciences:

Pharmacokinetics: Study of a substance's movement through the body

Pharmacodynamics: Study of the effect of substances and the mechanisms of action

Pharmaceutics: Concerned with use of medicinal substances

Pharmacoeconomics: Economics of pharmaceutical substances

The answer is **(B)**

Solution 304

If a user develops a tolerance to a specific substance, they will also likely have a tolerance to other substances in the same classification. In this scenario, since the morphine is similar heroin, the user already has a tolerance. This is called cross-tolerance.

The answer is **(D)**

Solution 305

In this scenario the user psychologically has a need to use the substances and cannot function properly without them. This is a sign of psychological dependence. Physical dependence is followed by withdrawal symptoms.

The answer is **(B)**

Solution 306

A cough preparation substance is considered schedule 5 if it has less than 200 mg per 100 ml.

The answer is **(C)**

Solution 307

Adolescents have not yet developed the ability to make sound judgements and they may rely on decisions based on emotion or satisfaction. This can often be attributed to the prefrontal cortex which has a role in judgement and the controlling of emotions.

The answer is (A)

Solution 308

Research shows that the faster a substance reaches the brain, the more addicting it will be.

The answer is (B)

Solution 309

Serotonin helps to control the body's mood, sleep, sexual desire, and appetite. One of the drugs that affects the neurotransmitter is Ecstasy.

The answer is (C)

Solution 310

Classical conditioning is when a stimulus is presented and then followed by an action to associate the two together. The subject begins with an unconditioned response but over time will change to a conditioned response by understanding the association.

The answer is (A)

Solution 311

When a client assumes certain thoughts or feelings of another based on certain perceptions, the client is using projection.

The answer is (C)

Solution 312

The mascot often will use humor as a way to distract from the situation, ease tension, or mask the pain.

The answer is **(D)**

Solution 313

Dialectical Behavior Therapy is based on understanding the diametric nature of things. For instance, to understand light you must understand darkness as well. This is often used for suicidal clients. The four primary modules are:

1. Mindfulness
2. Distress Tolerance
3. Interpersonal Effectiveness
4. Emotional Regulation

The answer is **(A)**

Solution 314

The A-B-C theory includes <u>A</u>ctivating events, <u>B</u>eliefs related to those events, and emotional and behavioral <u>C</u>onsequences. It can also be expanded to Disputing intervention, The Effect of disputing intervention, and the Feeling resulting from the effect.

The answer is **(C)**

Solution 315

To prevent relapse, it is important for an individual to obtain the necessary skills to abstain and be prepared for potential triggers. It is not as heavily related to an individual's determination as it is typically perceived.

The answer is **(B)**

Solution 316

The primary diagnosis can be either related to substances or mental health, but is identified by whichever comes first in the client's life. The secondary diagnosis is whichever is identified second.

The answer is **(C)**

Solution 317

Dysthymia is also known as persistent depressive disorder in which the client has two years of depressive characteristics but cannot be classified as major depressive disorder.

The answer is **(C)**

Solution 318

An individual who has social fears due to being judged and avoids social situations is suffering from avoidant personality disorder.

The answer is **(A)**

Solution 319

DSM-5 provides criteria for evaluating depression. The client must meet five of those listed. The criteria includes significant weight loss, diminished pleasure in activities, fatigue and others.

The answer is **(B)**

Solution 320

The half-life of a substance is the time it takes for the body to eliminate half of the concentration of a substance from initial administration. The half-life for an individual can vary on many factors such as weight or biology but the type of substance administration will affect the half-life with relative consistency. Smoking and injecting provide a quick peak of concentration to the brain so the half-life is relatively fast. Snorting takes more time but ingestion is the slowest process and therefore the longest half-life.

The answer is **(D)**

Solution 321

There are three stages in the ARISE Method which is an acronym for A Relational Sequence for Engagement. Stage three only occurs if the network will take action based on the individual not agreeing to seek treatment.

The answer is **(B)**

Solution 322

There are three broad categories of stressors: external factors, internal distress, and transitional stress. Transitional stress is a change in the fundamental elements of an individual's life. This may be divorce, job change, a move etc.

The answer is **(A)**

Solution 323

Group therapy and mutual support groups are both ways for the individual to grow and learn but the processes are very different. Mutual support groups are more open in both size and membership and helps to empower change in the individual. This is in contrast to therapy in which the group is the agent of change.

The answer is **(B)**

Solution 324

There are 5 stages of group development:

1. Forming: Initial introductions and familiarity
2. Storming: Chaotic development of the group dynamics
3. Norming: Norms are agreed upon
4. Performing: The group is able to reach objectives
5. Adjourning: Moving on from the group structure

The answer is **(D)**

Solution 325

When treating a client for a relapse, it is not recommended to limit the client's options. Providing the client with flexibility will help them to not feel trapped or forced into a decision.

The answer is **(B)**

Solution 326

The twelfth step is "Having had a spiritual awakening as the result of these steps, we tried to carry this message to alcoholics and to practice these principals in all our affairs."

The answer is **(D)**

Solution 327

If a counselor needs to understand something better or is unsure of something the client says, they can employ clarification. This is marked by asking questions such as "can you explain…." or "could you clarify what you mean by that?"

The answer is **(B)**

Solution 328

Transference and countertransference both refer to the projecting of feelings or attitudes. Transference is the client on the counselor. Countertransference is the opposite.

The answer is **(D)**

Solution 329

An individual who progresses through the stages of sexual identity acceptance begins with confusion or denial, then begins to entertain the idea. This is followed by self-identification and then acceptance. The level at which the thought is being entertained is identity comparison.

The answer is **(B)**

Solution 330

Drug tests must be taken when they are requested. Any refusal will result in the same consequences as if it was a positive result.

The answer is **(B)**

Solution 331

The advanced stage is marked with positive change in one's lifestyle such as healthy relationships, spiritual programs, or a balanced life. This is where the client begins to break away from the dependence on the treatment facility.

The answer is **(A)**

Solution 332

Adolescents have a specific set of character traits that can cause complications during treatment. These may include low self-esteem, poor self-image, a rebellious nature, peer pressure and others. A private lifestyle however is more often attributed to older individuals.

The answer is **(C)**

Solution 333

Research shows that around 70% of women have suffered abuse physically or sexually and have a substance abuse disorder.

The answer is **(C)**

Solution 334

While everyone is at risk, some populations are more so than others. These include minorities, gay men, and heterosexual women.

The answer is **(C)**

Solution 335

An individual who recovers from Hepatitis C, unlike B, can become re-infected. Those who have B can develop an immunity.

The answer is **(B)**

Solution 336

One who identifies with a dominant culture is accultured.

Bi-cultural is an individual who identifies with their own ethnic group and the culture in which they live.

Culturally immersed people actively reflect a pro-minority stance.

Traditional-interpersonal people accept his or her identity as it simply is.

The answer is **(A)**

Solution 337

There are three separate parts of the mind:

Id: The animal instinct portion. Emotional, aggressive, often selfish

Superego: Morally driven conscience portion

Ego: Mediation between Id and Superego

The answer is **(C)**

Solution 338

There is a variety of types of ethics which relate to different aspects of decision making. Some include:

- Principle Ethics: Societal and personal morals
- Positive Ethics: Making decisions based on aspirational thinking. Doing what is best for a client
- Values Ethics: Core beliefs that guide a person
- Virtue Ethics: The idea of establishing what is right and what is wrong

Values ethics are concerned with an individual understanding who they are as a person.

The answer is **(C)**

Solution 339

To be able to evaluate, assess and take action, the ethical dilemma must first be identified and examined to understand the specifics of the situation.

The answer is **(C)**

Solution 340

Bartering may take place but must be requested by the client, be legal according to law, and agreed upon by contract prior. There is no limit on the agreed value.

The answer is **(D)**

Solution 341

Cognitive-behavior therapy explores the client's thoughts, emotions, and behaviors and tries to restructure automatic responses to stimuli so that they may make better decisions.

The answer is **(A)**

Solution 342

For a third-party observation of any client interaction to occur, the client must provide written consent. The exceptions are for educational purposes such as students in field placement or agency trainees.

The answer is **(A)**

Solution 343

The counselor does not have to sign off on the disclosure as a required element.

The answer is **(B)**

Solution 344

Cultural humility is a lifelong assessment of one's self from a diversity perspective and allows the individual to better develop interpersonal relationships.

The answer is **(C)**

Solution 345

Clinical supervision is in place to:

1. Protect the welfare of the client
2. Help the supervisee grow
3. Monitor performance
4. Promote self-supervision

The supervisor does not provide personal counseling

The answer is **(D)**

Solution 346

There are 3 levels with a 4th being an acknowledgment of reaching level 3 across all domains. The progression begins with level 1 in which the counselor is fully dependent and has limited training. Level 2 is marked by moving away from the dependence. At level 3 the counselor begins to use a personalized approach to the work.

The answer is **(C)**

Solution 347

The cognitive-behavioral-based supervision theory focuses on the consequences that result from what the client thinks and feels about the issues presented and what the supervisee thinks and feels about the therapeutic alliance.

The answer is **(A)**

Solution 348

There is a differentiation between violations with and without harm done. If there is no evidence of harm done, the appropriate action is to first try to resolve the issue informally.

The answer is **(B)**

Solution 349

Vicarious liability is when a supervisor may be responsible for violations by providing incorrect or improper advice. They can provide advice to seek legal counsel if warranted.

The answer is **(A)**

Solution 350

There are many things to avoid doing to ensure matters do not get worse during an investigation. These include seeking legal counsel for any actions or meetings and not making any changes to existing documents. There should be no separate contact made with the person who filed the complaint.

The answer is **(A)**

Solution 351

Incentives may be provided to a client but they must be agreed to and disclosed to the client before participation begins.

The answer is **(A)**

Solution 352

Boundary issues are disruptions to the professional relationship. Boundary violations are actions which actually will or potentially cause harm to the client. A boundary crossing is an action which deviates from the standards of practice for a professional relationship but cause no actual harm. This may come in the form of a dual relationship as described in the example.

The answer is **(C)**

Solution 353

A Peer Recovery Support Specialist is someone who can help to support and motivate the individual progressing through recovery. They do not however provide specific direction to the client.

The answer is **(A)**

Solution 354

There are four transdisciplinary foundations:

1. Understanding Addiction
2. Treatment Knowledge
3. Application to Practice
4. Professional Readiness

Understanding models of addiction is classified under foundation I.

The answer is **(A)**

Solution 355

With a general progression through the recovery phases, an individual will reasonably expect to reach the maintenance phase after 18 months.

The answer is **(C)**

Solution 356

The DAST 20 provides 20 questions each being worth one point. Severe is the highest indication and would have a range of 16-20.

The answer is **(D)**

Solution 357

The discharge and continuing care plan should detail what the reason for leaving is and how the client will move forward. There is no longer a need for compliance checks if they are leaving.

The answer is **(B)**

Solution 358

Person-centered therapy is based on the flipping of roles for recovery meaning the client will be the main source of invoking change. The three main attitudes for a counselor are:

1. Congruence: The ability to match internal feeling and thoughts to external expression
2. Unconditional positive regard: Unconditional acceptance in caring
3. Accurate empathetic understanding: A deep understanding of the client's world

The answer is **(A)**

Solution 359

The client has an idealized world in her head which is unachievable and not reality. She then creates a fictional goal that guides her behavior. This is fictional finalism.

The answer is **(D)**

Solution 360

With co-occurring disorders, the treatment plan must include an approach to the interaction of the two treatments. They can be:

- Parallel: Occurring at the same time but separate
- Sequential: Treatment for one and then the next when the first is complete
- Integrated: A single comprehensive treatment

The answer is **(A)**

Solution 361

The stages progress in the order of emotional relapse, mental relapse, and then physical.

The answer is **(A)**

Solution 362

While following through with the termination is important if necessary, the client needs to be given the opportunity to change so that they may be given the chance to rectify, if possible, the reason for the referral.

The answer is **(A)**

Solution 363

Dimension 2 is concerned with the individual's health history and current assessment of physical appearance and condition.

The answer is **(B)**

Solution 364

Nonverbal cues are an essential part to physical and mental assessments. Anger can be manifested in actions such as lowered eyebrows, tight lips, or head shaking. Open arms while not an indicator of the opposite, does not generally show anger.

The answer is **(C)**

Solution 365

There are typically three phases in which clients progress toward attempting suicide. The first is expression of suicidal thoughts as per the indication in the example. Then it progresses to devising a plan for suicide. Then action is taken to carry out the plan such as settling affairs or preparing to say goodbye to loved ones.

The answer is **(B)**

Solution 366

The need statement is separate from the goal statement which indicates the vision of the end product for the client.

The answer is **(C)**

Solution 367

Progress noted are the counselor's personal account of what is taking place and should be documented for each interaction with the client.

The answer is **(A)**

Solution 368

A multidisciplinary addiction treatment team can be composed of any members who have a role in treating the client's substance abuse. These may include many professionals such as pharmacy, therapists, peer support, mental health, and many others

The answer is **(D)**

Solution 369

In general, most models of group therapy stages follow a similar progression: orientation, conflict, openness, and closing. Conflict will occur after introductions and as the group dynamic is forming. For the Stokes and Tate model this is the groundwork stage.

The answer is **(B)**

Solution 370

An action response is one that is meant to illicit a response from the client that will lead them into providing further or meaningful insight. These are different from listening and attending which show the counselor is listening and understanding the interaction.

The answer is **(A)**

Solution 371

Self-disclosure can be a difficult evaluation of whether or not to proceed. In general, if any of the following are answered as "No" then the disclosure is not considered appropriate:

1. Is the counselor comfortable with the disclosure?
2. Will this help the client?
3. Will this help the counselor-client connection?
4. Will this help the client progress in treatment?

Despite thinking the story can help the client, if the counselor is uncomfortable it is not recommended to proceed.

The answer is **(B)**

Solution 372

A conditioned response is when a different action is taken than originally to a stimulus after some conditioning to change.

The answer is **(B)**

Solution 373

Screening is the evaluation of the potential presence of substance abuse and whether or not the subject should advance to assessment. Assessment is a more detailed evaluation of the condition and severity of substance use.

The answer is **(B)**

Solution 374

A follow-up drug test is for individuals who have previously tested positive, have returned to duty, and may now be subject to additional testing.

The answer is **(C)**

Solution 375

There are different types of ethical theories that provide a foundation for decision making. They are:

- Humanistic ethics: Understanding the value and worth of people by allowing them to have freedom of decision making based on critical thinking
- Clinical pragmatism: Includes an interpersonal process of assessment and consensus building
- Situational ethics: Understanding that each situation needs to be evaluated for moral direction
- Religious ethics: What is right and wrong based on the direction of a religion

The answer is **(A)**

Solution 376

There are a number of different treatment options which must be chosen based on the individual. Outpatient means the patient is no longer in a treatment facility but at their own residence. In intensive outpatient there is scheduled structured treatments at frequent intervals.

The answer is **(D)**

Solution 377

Different substances have different effects on the physical state of the brain. Some will elicit a fabricated reaction as if they were a neurotransmitter. These are called agonists. Others will block the reaction and are called antagonists.

The answer is **(B)**

Solution 378

While the percentage of alcohol varies for individual drinks, the U.S. standard is 12 ounces of beer, 1.5 oz of 80-proof spirits and 5 ounces of wine.

The answer is **(B)**

Solution 379

For an alcoholic, many of their daily calories are taken by the alcohol itself and daily food caloric intake is reduced. It is estimated that 50% of the user's calories are from alcohol and the food intake can be less than 1000 daily calories and as low as 300 in some cases.

The answer is **(B)**

Solution 380

Of the options listed, Disulfiram will create a negative reaction to consuming of alcohol.

The answer is **(A)**

Solution 381

Opiates include any naturally occurring substances extracted from opium. These include morphine, codeine, thebaine.

Opioids are naturally, synthetic, or semi-synthetic substance which includes opium.

All opiates are opioids but not vice versa. Hydrocodone is a semi-synthetic version and therefore is an opioid but not opiate.

The answer is **(D)**

Solution 382

Most substances must be metabolized in the liver and this is source of the strong association of substance abuse and liver disorders. Inhalants since they are breathed in through the respiratory system, mostly pass through the lungs.

The answer is **(B)**

Solution 383

Of those listed, ether, chloroform, and nitrous oxides are classified as an anesthetic due to their ability to reduce the sensation to pain. Butane is a volatile solvent often found in lighters.

The answer is **(D)**

Solution 384

Inhalants can be administered in a variety of ways. The easiest is sniffing, spraying, or snorting through the nose. Bagging is when an inhalant is sprayed into a bag and then inhaled. Vaporizing can be done to alcohol to inhale the fumes. Injecting, since inhalants are gaseous, is not an option for administration.

The answer is **(B)**

Solution 385

Research has determined that over half (about 57%) of children ages 12-17 who abuse opioids obtained them from a friend or relative.

The answer is **(A)**

Solution 386

Cannabis plants have a powdery resin called kief. When these are collected and pressed together, the concentrate is called Hashish. Shatter is solidified hash oil and BHO (Butane Hash Oil) is an extraction of the THC from cannabis by spraying butane on the buds.

The answer is **(A)**

Solution 387

Binge drinking is classified as any consumption of 5 or more standard drinks for men and 4 or more standard drinks for women on the same occasion defined as a 2-hour time period.

The answer is **(D)**

Solution 388

Caffeine is found in coffee beans, tea, and cocoa. It is also found in the plants yerba mate, yoco, and guarana. Cheroot is a type of cigar in India containing tobacco.

The answer is **(B)**

Solution 389

Crack is a smokable form of cocaine which is mixed with baking soda and water. It contains many of the characteristics of cocaine but some of the differences are that it is smoked causing a quicker effect.

The answer is **(C)**

Solution 390

Privileged communication keeps the conversations held with clients and health professionals confidential in a court of law. The exceptions include:

- Court ordered exam: If the court determines an evaluation needs to be performed that information will be shared
- Harm to others: If there is a reason to believe by the counselor that harm may be done, the information can be shared
- Abuse to other: If there is reason to believe someone is being abused, the information can be released
- Health placed in issue: If a mental state of being is a factor in a court case, there are scenarios where the information can be accessed

Dual relationships, while not ethical, do not break privileged communication

The answer is **(C)**

Solution 391

When evaluating tools, the results should be reviewed to ensure the test is providing the intended result and that it produces it on a consistent basis. Validity refers to the instruments ability to measure its intended purpose. Content validity refers to the appropriateness of the content within the instrument. Reliability on the other hand, is consistent measure of the instrument's intention.

The answer is **(C)**

Solution 392

Despite the use of technology, the State and Federal Laws that apply at the counselor's location will still apply for the interaction.

The answer is **(A)**

Solution 393

Adolescents may have a strong hesitation to providing honest answers for fear of punishment. It is often beneficial to provide time where the parents or guardian are not in the room and that the adolescent is protected from any consequences based on the results. You do not want to give off the impression that drinking is normal behavior that should be brushed off.

The answer is **(B)**

Solution 394

Alcohol abuse has a strong economic impact due to the need for treatment and the damage it causes. The most prevalent source of economic loss is wage loss due to alcohol-related illness.

The answer is **(B)**

Solution 395

Second hand smoke has severe risks and is responsible for thousands of deaths each year. There is no risk-free exposure to second hand smoke.

The answer is **(D)**

Solution 396

Motivational incentives are rewards to help a client maintain the path to recovery. Empathy while important to the overall process is not specifically related to the process of implementing motivational incentives.

The answer is **(C)**

Solution 397

Smokeless tobacco has many of the same hazards as cigarettes. There is, however, less identified chemicals in smokeless tobacco. However, cancer and other health risks still exist.

The answer is **(B)**

Solution 398

While an addiction counselor does not specifically treat depression, it could be playing a key role in the substance abuse disorder. A depressed person will tend to have certain viewpoints on the world around them. These include jumping to conclusions quickly, looking only at the negatives and seeing the world only as one extreme or the other without considering nuance. They also tend to be disbelieving of others or not seeing them as genuine.

The answer is **(B)**

Solution 399

There are situations where there is a low to moderate risk for adolescents who have indicated drinking in the past. For those at the age of 10 or even 11, any indication of drinking should be treated with a high level of concern

The answer is **(D)**

Solution 400

SAMSHA TAP 21 has eight practice dimensions:

1. Clinical Evaluation
2. Treatment Planning
3. Referral
4. Service Coordination
5. Counseling
6. Client, Family, and Community Education
7. Documentation
8. Professional and Ethical Responsibility

Competency 48 refers to the treatment plan

The answer is **(B)**

Solution 401

Empathy is an important part of the therapeutic alliance with a client. Many times, the client needs to be understood fully so that progress can be made. Sympathy is more concerned with compassion and having feelings in relation to the client's situation. Empathy takes effort and investigation whereas sympathy is more or less automatic human behavior.

The answer is **(B)**

Solution 402

While there are some cases, antidepressants in general are not addictive. The appropriate type used cannot be predicted but after a reasonable amount of time, another can be used if there is no progress.

The answer is **(C)**

Solution 403

When helping for pain there are a number of medications available. Many of which are not habit forming but some that do include muscle relaxants, benzodiazepines, and cannabinoids.

The answer is **(B)**

Solution 404

While research has not been able to accurately identify specific amounts or times when the risk occurs, there is no research that indicates a safe time or amount of alcohol to be drank during pregnancy.

The answer is **(A)**

Solution 405

Hallucinogens can be administered in a number of ways including pills, liquid, snorting, injection, or inhaling. Those which are commonly brewed into tea include ayahuasca, psilocybin, salvia, and peyote.

The answer is **(A)**

Solution 406

There is a range of reasons why a person will not enter treatment. They can be classified into the following:

- Intrapersonal: Individual mental or health issues
- Interpersonal: Relationship issues
- Sociocultural: Social factors or stigmas
- Structural: The characteristics and limitation of the treatment program
- Systemic: Larger system issues such as federal or state agencies

The answer is **(D)**

Solution 407

Women tend to be more likely to suffer from PTSD and the duration can be twice as long.

The answer is **(A)**

Solution 408

Parental supervision has a strong impact on the child's susceptibility to using substances. The recommended practice is to have clear and consistent rules as well as strong communication. Showing active concern by checking with a child is also recommended.

The answer is **(C)**

Solution 409

An overdose due to cocaine will incur serious medical conditions which need to be addressed such as stroke or heart failure. There is no medication that can have a positive effect on the person once overdose has occurred.

The answer is **(A)**

Solution 410

Drunk drivers will often have many instances of driving under the influence before being caught. This number is sometimes estimated to be around 80 instances.

The answer is **(D)**

Solution 411

E-cigarettes may have a perception that they can help people quit smoking, but they are not one of the seven approved FDA products.

The answer is **(B)**

Solution 412

The main theory behind client-centered therapy is that the client has the ability to complete the path to recovery but the counselor must establish the relationship that allows the client to achieve this. Therefore, it is strongly geared towards developing the rapport and relationship upfront.

The answer is **(A)**

Solution 413

Within the precontemplation stage of change, there are further classifications:

- Resigned precontemplation: Feels that change would be hopeless or too exhausting
- Rationalizing precontemplation: Not me mentality. Substances are not actually a problem for the user
- Reluctant precontemplation: Lack knowledge or the actual personal impact
- Rebellious precontemplation: Afraid of losing control over their lives

The answer is **(A)**

Solution 414

Men have a threshold over which there is a significant increase in the risk of liver disease at more than 13 drinks.

The answer is **(B)**

Solution 415

If a client and a counselor reach an impasse for the determination of goals there are several options. The counselor can refer the client to another unless they are willing to commit. They can negotiate to an acceptable level. Or approximation is allowing the client to make a step in the right direction in hopes of achieving other goals in the future.

The answer is **(C)**

Solution 416

A standard drink of hard liquor is 1.5 ounces of 80 proof.

The answer is **(C)**

Solution 417

The matrix model is an intensive outpatient treatment which is highly structured and has been shown to be effective specifically for stimulants but for other substances as well.

The answer is **(A)**

Solution 418

The "treatment gap" as it is termed, is the difference between those who would greatly benefit from receiving treatment to those who actually do. This is a small number estimated around 10%.

The answer is **(A)**

Solution 419

Fentanyl is a stronger and more potent version of morphine that is used to treat extreme pain or chronic pain in which morphine is not working. It can be prescribed by a licensed physician.

The answer is **(B)**

Solution 420

Brief therapy as the name suggests is shorter sessions that accelerate the process. These are good for a large number of clients by nature of requiring less time and a greater or already established client commitment. Despite the shortened timeframe, there will be well defined short term and long-term goals.

The answer is **(B)**

Solution 421

It is important to understand the entire picture of treatment for a client. If any new medication is to be taken it should be evaluated to ensure it fits into the treatment plan.

The answer is **(D)**

Solution 422

Hallucinogens mostly do not cause a physical dependence except in some cases with PCP. The use patterns are more isolated than other substances.

The answer is **(A)**

Solution 423

Research indicates that while it is important for the client to eventually be engaged and motivated, the initial mindset entering treatment does not have a correlation to success rates.

The answer is **(A)**

Solution 424

Non-controlled substances are those which fall outside of the DEA schedules and are determined to have a lower level of risk. These can be over the counter or prescription which includes treatment for high blood pressure, diabetes, or bacterial infections. Amoxicillin is an antibiotic used to treat infections.

The answer is **(A)**

Solution 425

The need for empathy in counseling makes it difficult to sometimes separate what happens professionally from the personal emotions of a counselor. A constant wearing on mental toughness can have negative effects on the counselor's mental state. This is a result of compassion fatigue.

The answer is **(D)**

Solution 426

The gateway drug hypothesis states that a user who has experimented with a substance will be more likely to use a higher risk substance due to familiarity from the original use. These are most often alcohol, marijuana, and tobacco.

The answer is **(B)**

Solution 427

Besides the typical urine test there are some more intensive and accurate tests:

- Thin layer chromatography: Uses a thin layer of plastic with a porous silica material to detect a wide range of substances
- Immunoassay test: Introduction of antibodies which rapidly detect the presence of substances
- Gas chromatography: Measures chemicals by segregation and measurement of speeds

The answer is **(B)**

Solution 428

Ketamine and PCP are the only classified hallucinogens which have a recognized medical use. Ketamine can be used for anesthesia purposes.

The answer is **(C)**

Solution 429

Reverse tolerance is where a lower than normal dose can begin to cause the desired effect. This can occur at times after repeated use of amphetamines.

The answer is **(A)**

Solution 430

A treatment facility that is not equipped to properly treat a specific client should not provide inappropriate care. There is an ethical obligation however to ensure the client is placed in a more suited facility.

The answer is **(C)**

Solution 431

This question is made to convey the idea that there are seemingly endless ways that substance users can hide them or use them. Writing utensils, food, books, cars, clothing and many others can be made as means to facilitate drug use

The answer is **(D)**

Solution 432

While it is often perceived that marijuana does not have detrimental effects, there is a number of issues that have been shown to be linked with heavy use. These include lower self-worth, lower graduation and employment rates, and even a drop in IQ by potentially 8 points. Marijuana is linked however to relieving pain.

The answer is **(C)**

Solution 433

Of first-time users of marijuana, about 75% are adolescents. This means that this age range is a crucial time in the decision to use substances or not.

The answer is **(C)**

Solution 434

A complaint should be filed as soon as possible. The cutoff is 180 days after an incident however the time frame can be extended due to a "good cause".

The answer is **(D)**

Solution 435

The transition from prison back into a normal life can be difficult due to the reduction in structure. It is easy for an individual to now regress to familiar situations or people that will hinder progress. It is important that the basic needs of these individuals are met such as safe and appropriate housing. It is common for those released from prison to use transitional housing to help create a strong foundation.

The answer is **(B)**

Solution 436

There are five levels that a counselor can progress through in regards to the relationship with the family of a client:

1. Minimal emphasis – The counselor only provides logistical information on a broad basis to all family members involved
2. Information and advice – The counselor begins to interact and engage with the family by providing information and answering specific questions
3. Feelings and support – The counselor is able to provide guidance and advice by knowing and understanding the family dynamics
4. Systematic assessment and brief intervention – Actively engaging family members in the process
5. Family therapy – Engagement in therapy as a family

The answer is **(C)**

Solution 437

The diagnostic criteria includes observing two or more of the following:

1. Delusions
2. Hallucinations
3. Gross disorganizations
4. Disorganized speech
5. Negative symptoms

The answer is **(B)**

Solution 438

It is advantageous to reduce the number of excuses a client may make to avoid treatment, especially in the beginning stages. Having a flexible schedule for sessions will decrease the likelihood of conflicting priorities.

The answer is **(A)**

Solution 439

There are many ways to use cannabis however cotton balls are more often associated with injections which is not associated with marijuana.

The answer is **(B)**

Solution 440

DXM is a hallucinogen commonly found in cough suppressants and expectorants.

The answer is **(A)**

Solution 441

In general, there is a cultural embracing of silence in Native American people that differs from many other perceptions.

The answer is **(D)**

Solution 442

Brief interventions are directed at nondependent individuals or those with an identified motivation to change. Those who fall outside this would need a more robust treatment than what brief ones offer.

The answer is **(D)**

Solution 443

Congeners are chemical compounds commonly found in dark liquors such as whisky that have shown to contribute to hangovers. This is the basis for people recommending clear liquors to avoid hangovers.

The answer is **(B)**

Solution 444

The client is exhibiting behavior that is a regression back to a cycle of drug seeking behavior. A relapse is a return to substance use but is an isolated incident. Recidivism occurs when there is a clear pattern of behavior that shows a cycle of substance abuse actions.

The answer is **(B)**

Solution 445

There is many factors going into the success of the use antidepressants but there is a range of research that indicates success about half of the time.

The answer is **(C)**

Solution 446

The amount of alcohol that an adolescent needs to consume to be classified as binge drinking than is less than for those of adults. Gender also is a factor. For girls ages 12-17, the number of drinks in a short time period to be considered binging is 3. For boys however it changes from 3 to 5 as the person grows older.

The answer is **(C)**

Solution 447

Attention Deficit Hyperactivity Disorder is marked with a lack of ability to focus or concentrate. The talking is an indicator of the need to be constantly engaged and a lack of patience.

The answer is **(A)**

Solution 448

Despite Marijuana being perceived as less harmful, it is often found to be associated with car crashes.

The answer is **(A)**

Solution 449

Drug cultures can be based on any number of commonalities. It can be political, social, drug type, gender, race, and many others. In this situation the drug culture that the client ascribes to has common interest in art and the type of drug. There is no indication that gender is a defining characteristic.

The answer is **(B)**

Solution 450

There are times when a client does not want to share information for fear of what may happen. A lack of understanding of confidentiality is a common fear for undocumented works due to the potential for deportation. The protections the client has should be clearly identified.

The answer is **(A)**

Answer Key

1	C	41	A	81	D	121	A	161	A	201	D	241	B	281	C
2	D	42	B	82	D	122	B	162	A	202	A	242	D	282	A
3	C	43	D	83	A	123	A	163	B	203	B	243	B	283	A
4	B	44	B	84	D	124	A	164	D	204	C	244	A	284	B
5	D	45	B	85	B	125	B	165	A	205	D	245	A	285	C
6	A	46	C	86	B	126	A	166	C	206	A	246	D	286	A
7	D	47	C	87	B	127	D	167	B	207	D	247	A	287	C
8	A	48	C	88	D	128	B	168	B	208	C	248	D	288	B
9	B	49	A	89	B	129	C	169	B	209	D	249	A	289	D
10	C	50	A	90	A	130	A	170	A	210	C	250	D	290	A
11	B	51	D	91	D	131	A	171	A	211	D	251	B	291	D
12	C	52	A	92	A	132	B	172	B	212	A	252	A	292	D
13	A	53	B	93	D	133	D	173	C	213	A	253	A	293	B
14	C	54	B	94	C	134	C	174	C	214	C	254	B	294	B
15	C	55	C	95	B	135	D	175	A	215	C	255	A	295	B
16	D	56	C	96	B	136	A	176	C	216	B	256	A	296	B
17	A	57	B	97	A	137	D	177	D	217	B	257	B	297	C
18	D	58	A	98	D	138	C	178	D	218	A	258	A	298	C
19	C	59	A	99	C	139	D	179	B	219	D	259	A	299	D
20	C	60	B	100	B	140	B	180	D	220	B	260	C	300	B
21	D	61	B	101	A	141	C	181	B	221	A	261	D		
22	A	62	D	102	A	142	B	182	A	222	B	262	A		
23	A	63	C	103	A	143	D	183	B	223	D	263	A		
24	C	64	D	104	C	144	D	184	A	224	A	264	D		
25	C	65	A	105	B	145	C	185	C	225	D	265	C		
26	A	66	A	106	D	146	C	186	C	226	B	266	D		
27	C	67	D	107	A	147	A	187	A	227	A	267	B		
28	D	68	A	108	D	148	A	188	A	228	D	268	B		
29	C	69	D	109	B	149	C	189	B	229	A	269	A		
30	B	70	C	110	D	150	B	190	D	230	C	270	C		
31	A	71	B	111	B	151	C	191	D	231	A	271	D		
32	A	72	D	112	D	152	A	192	A	232	B	272	B		
33	D	73	A	113	A	153	D	193	B	233	B	273	B		
34	A	74	D	114	C	154	A	194	A	234	C	274	C		
35	D	75	A	115	A	155	C	195	B	235	A	275	A		
36	A	76	B	116	B	156	A	196	C	236	D	276	C		
37	B	77	C	117	D	157	D	197	C	237	B	277	D		
38	A	78	B	118	B	158	A	198	A	238	A	278	D		
39	C	79	A	119	A	159	B	199	D	239	A	279	B		
40	B	80	A	120	C	160	C	200	B	240	B	280	B		

301	A	341	A	381	D	421	D
302	C	342	A	382	B	422	A
303	B	343	B	383	D	423	A
304	D	344	C	384	B	424	A
305	B	345	D	385	A	425	D
306	C	346	C	386	A	426	B
307	A	347	A	387	D	427	B
308	B	348	B	388	B	428	C
309	C	349	A	389	C	429	A
310	A	350	A	390	C	430	C
311	C	351	A	391	C	431	D
312	D	352	C	392	A	432	C
313	A	353	A	393	B	433	C
314	C	354	A	394	B	434	D
315	B	355	C	395	D	435	B
316	C	356	D	396	C	436	C
317	C	357	B	397	B	437	B
318	A	358	A	398	B	438	A
319	B	359	D	399	D	439	B
320	D	360	A	400	B	440	A
321	B	361	A	401	B	441	D
322	A	362	A	402	C	442	D
323	B	363	C	403	B	443	B
324	D	364	B	404	A	444	B
325	B	365	A	405	A	445	C
326	D	366	C	406	D	446	C
327	B	367	A	407	A	447	A
328	D	368	D	408	C	448	A
329	B	369	B	409	A	449	B
330	B	370	A	410	D	450	A
331	A	371	B	411	B		
332	C	372	B	412	A		
333	C	373	B	413	A		
334	C	374	C	414	B		
335	B	375	A	415	C		
336	A	376	D	416	C		
337	C	377	B	417	A		
338	C	378	B	418	A		
339	C	379	B	419	B		
340	D	380	A	420	B		

Thank You Again for Your Purchase!

What Did You Think of the Practice Exams?

It is a long and difficult road to passing and we are extremely grateful you chose us to help along the way. We hope that it added value and efficiency to your studying. We are here for any questions or concerns you may have and we will respond quickly if you email us at:

Bovabooks@gmail.com

If you enjoyed this book it would help greatly if you have the time to **leave a positive review on our Amazon product page**. Reviews help to support small businesses like ours.

References

Getting Ready to Test: A Review/Preparation Manual for Drug and Alcohol Credentialing Examinations; DLC, LLC; 8th Edition January 2017 Revision

Study Guide IC&RC Alcohol and Drug Counselor Certification Exam; Pamela Waters, Gail Dixon, Pamela Baston; Third Edition 2016

Basics of Addiction Counseling Desk Reference. Modules 1-3; NAADAC March 2018

Made in the USA
Las Vegas, NV
10 June 2021